BREADSTICKS PANIN

DOUGHNUTS BIALYS

PIZZAS FOCACC

TARTLETS NAAN BAGUETT

PIZZAS

DOUGHNUTS

BIALYS PIADINAS NAAN

PRETZELS

FLATBREAD DOUGHNUTS PRETZELS NAAN

CHALLAH PIADINAS

PIZZETTAS NAAN

PIZZA DOUGH

100 Delicious, Unexpected Recipes

By Gabi Moskowitz

Photographs by Frankie Frankeny

EGG&DART.PRESS

Acknowledgments:

To Pam Falk for believing in me from the very beginning, and whose ability to transform my fuzzy brainstorms into a beautiful product is one of a kind.

To Gretchen Scoble, whose beautiful design inspires me every time I look at it.

To Frankie Frankeny and Fanny Pan, who made my food look mouthwatering and gorgeous.

To Marlene Koch, who believed my blog deserved to be a book, and helped me make it happen.

To my mother, who encouraged me to write from the time I learned how to do it; my father, who bestowed in me a strong sense of perseverance, as well as a deep love of pizza; and my brother Jeremy, on whom I got to practice my early (and often terrible) cooking.

To my wonderful friends, family and readers whose support was instrumental in creating this book, specifically Andrew Kaufteil, Ady Thakur, Caitlin Doty, Carina Ost, Carrie Rice, Kristina Welzien, Laura Rumpf, Nada Perrone, Rebecca Kee, the Douglasses, the Gregers, the Rosses, the Brittons, the Bransten-Rumseys, the Wolkensteins, and the whole team at ZeroCater.

And to Evan, with whom I'd rather spend time than do just about anything.

© Dynamic Housewares Inc, 2013
Text © 2013 Gabi Moskowitz, 2013
Photographs © Frankie Frankeny, 2013

ISBN 978-09887731-1-0
Manufactured in China
Designed by Gretchen Scoble
10 9 8 7 6 5 4 3 2 1

EGG&DART PRESS

www.egganddartpress.com

For my mother

Contents

Introduction

In the fall of 2008, I was the brokest I have ever been.

I was in that all-too-common post-college, pre-professional-success, "what-the-heck-am-I-going-to-do-with-myself?" quarter-life crisis. In between jobs and on the cusp of figuring out my next move, I had lots of drive, tons of heart, and absolutely no money. Unfortunately, I also had—and have—expensive taste. Thanks to my wine country upbringing and residence in food-obsessed San Francisco, I just couldn't swallow the idea of eating badly (or even just blandly) as a means for saving money. No way.

Fortunately, I had food savvy. I set to work developing BrokeAssGourmet.com, the blog I maintain to this day, focusing on high-quality, low-budget meals that always cost less than $20 to make. I built a basic pantry (more on that later) and researched the best wines for the least bucks. I had found my calling. The blog was great, and quickly it took up most of my time. Still, it was awhile before it yielded any income. And there was still that matter of having to eat.

One afternoon, I was getting ready to go to a dinner party. My plan was to bring a large zip-top bag filled with the fresh, cheap pizza dough I had just made, along with little containers of tomato sauce, pesto, cheese, and other toppings. With these, I thought, people could make their own calzones and personal pizzas. It would be a fun, interactive way to cook. As I grabbed my keys and headed for the door, the friend who was hosting the dinner called me to cancel it.

"Great," I remember thinking. What was I going to do with three pounds of pizza dough? As it turned out, a lot.

That night, I had a friend come over, last minute, and we made pizza together. Easy and fresh, it was way better than delivery. But I still had a lot of dough left.

So the next morning, seeking something fun to make for brunch, I experimented with filling the dough with a mixture of butter, cinnamon, and sugar, rolling it up and then slicing and baking it into cinnamon rolls. Huge success. That night, I made Indian curry and ended up frying pieces of the dough into a quick and surprisingly authentic-tasting naan flatbread. And, still, there was more. I ate a pizza dough–based or dough-augmented meal every day for the next week. Clearly, I had stumbled upon something great.

And so my obsession with pizza dough was born.

Now, the number-one tip I give new cooks is to always keep a ball of fresh pizza dough on hand. As far as I'm concerned, it's the very best way to make sure you never go hungry. Because even if your fridge is nearly bare and even if your kitchen equipment is minimal, you can always make something special and delicious out of pizza dough. Leftovers transform into something brand new. Suddenly, the bottom-of-the-vegetable bin greens and that remaining whisper of Parmesan become a bistro-worthy piadina. Pizza dough can be the backbone of every meal of every day if you want it to be—it's just that versatile.

And it's quick and easy to make. Even on nights when I'm just too tired to bring myself to cook a whole meal, I can always pull out a disk of frozen pizza dough (stacked neatly with parchment paper between, tucked in my freezer), top it with whatever sauces, cheese, vegetables or meat I happen to have laying around, and call it a darn good dinner.

This book is merely a slice (ha! get it? slice!) of all the amazing things that can be done with this wonderful yeasted dough, and, thusly, should be treated as a basic template and not the end-all-be-all of what you can do with pizza dough. Try the recipes as presented a few times and then have fun experimenting with your own additions. Don't worry too much about doing things "exactly right," as pizza dough is forgiving. Chances are, if you use good ingredients and simple techniques, you'll be

as golden-brown as the bubbly cheese atop your margherita pie.

What I really want you to get is that every recipe in this book is based upon a simple dough—that of the humble pizza pie. I want this book to show you just how easy it is to make fresh, real food using simple techniques.

So start with the basic dough. Practice it, master it, love it, and let it love you. Make a pizza or two.

Then try experimenting with some of the dough variations. Make calzones with a garlic-herb crust (page 21), and homemade Bagels (page 54). Congratulate yourself on how easy and fast it was (feel free to let your friends think you slaved for hours though). Make dough a regular part of your cooking repertoire.

I invite you to fall recklessly, fearlessly in love with pizza dough. It is, after all, the perfect first love: it's flexible and versatile, simple to understand yet capable of complexity, very pretty and endlessly forgiving.

And, unlike many other first loves, I guarantee that your mother will love it, too.

—Gabi Moskowitz

The Pizza Dough Pantry

In my first book, *The BrokeAss Gourmet Cookbook*, I included a list known as "The $50 Pantry." In this book, since we're focusing on pizza dough, some of the ingredients are a little bit different. Here are some of the nonperishables you should keep on hand for the recipes in this book:

Flour. King Arthur is a great brand. Buy it in 5-pound bags and immediately transfer it to an airtight container to keep in your pantry. If you plan to make variations of the dough, you'll need whole-wheat flour, rye flour, and/or gluten-free all purpose flour.

Canned tomatoes. My very favorite brand is Muir Glen Fire-Roasted tomatoes. Buy the whole kind, crushed or chopped, and use them to make a quick tomato sauce. They're also great to have on hand for last-minute tomato soup. I generally buy canned crushed and chopped tomatoes.

Extra-virgin olive oil. Use something you like the taste of. You'll use it over and over again: in the dough itself, for greasing bowls and pans, in sauces, and for drizzling.

Garlic. Pizza without garlic is just sad! Buy whole heads of garlic (the pre-peeled kind changes its flavor when it oxidizes) and pull off cloves as you need them. Never use sprouted, mushy, or dried-out garlic.

Kosher salt. I like the semi-coarse kind, sold in large cartons, with a metal pour-spout. I also like using coarse sea salt, although finely ground table salt will always do.

Pepper (ideally in a grinder). Don't bother with pre-ground black pepper—it loses flavor quickly. Instead, grind your own black peppercorns, directly over the food you are adding it to.

White granulated sugar. This is a staple pantry ingredient, and it's great for activating yeast. Keep it in an airtight container in your pantry.

Yeast. You can always buy the 3-packet strips found in most baking aisles, but you may get better value from a screw-top jar. Keep it in the freezer to extend its life even further. I prefer active dry yeast (Fleischmann's is a trustworthy brand). Proof it in warm water with a pinch of sugar. This is what "wakes it up" and gets it to do its thing, making your dough rise.

Sauces and Spreads

You can spread nearly anything edible (even choco-late!) over pizza dough before cooking it and still end up with something delicious. Still, I have a few old favorites—sauces I use time and time again with my pizza dough. These are great to whip up big batches of, perhaps on a Sunday afternoon, and then freeze or store in sealed jars. They even make wonderful gifts in a decorative container with a pretty ribbon tied around it!

All that said, please note that store-bought sauces, spreads, tapenades and dips are all fine substitu-tions, so feel free to use them in place of the home-made ones called for in this book.

Fresh Basil Pesto

Fresh basil pesto is one of those foods that you've probably bought prepared, but once you make it fresh, you will find yourself making it again and again. Fresh lemon juice and zest brightens up the flavors and keeps your pesto tasting fresh for days.

PREP TIME: 10 to 15 minutes
TOTAL TIME: 10 to 15 minutes
YIELD: 1½ cups pesto

2 cups tightly packed fresh basil leaves

½ cup grated Parmesan

½ cup pine nuts

2 to 3 cloves garlic, peeled and ends removed

½ cup olive oil

Zest and juice of one lemon

Salt and freshly ground black pepper to taste

1. Pummel all ingredients using a mortar and pestle (add the basil gradually so it breaks down without creating a huge mess) until smooth.

2. Alternatively, place all ingredients except lemon juice and olive oil in a food processor or blender and stream in liquids as the machine runs. Process until smooth.

Roasted Tomato Sauce

PREP TIME: 15 minutes
TOTAL TIME: 1 hour
YIELD: About 5 cups sauce

3 pounds tomatoes (beefsteak or plum)

1 medium onion, halved and sliced ¼ inch thick

4 cloves garlic, peeled

2 tablespoons olive oil

Salt and freshly ground black pepper

1. Preheat oven to 425°F. Use a sharp paring knife to core the tomatoes. Cut tomatoes in half; transfer to one large (or two smaller) rimmed baking sheet(s); add onion and garlic.

2. Drizzle the oil over the tomato mixture and season it with the salt and pepper. Spread in a single layer (turn the tomatoes sliced-side-down). Roast until soft, about 45 minutes (a bit longer, if the tomatoes are very ripe).

3. Using tongs or your fingers, peel off tomato skins; discard. Transfer the mixture to a blender or food processor and pulse several times, until chunky.

4. Let cool completely before using.

Quick Tomato Sauce

PREP TIME: 10 minutes
TOTAL TIME: 40 minutes
YIELD: 3 cups sauce

1 tablespoon extra-virgin olive oil

1 onion, diced

6 cloves garlic, chopped

Three 15-ounce cans chopped tomatoes

1 large handful fresh basil leaves, chopped

1 large handful fresh flat-leaf parsley leaves, chopped

1. Heat olive oil in a large pot over medium heat. Add onion and garlic and cook just until fragrant, about 1 minute.

2. Add the tomatoes, basil, and parsley. Stir and cover.

3. Cook for 8 to 10 minutes or until tomatoes have broken down.

4. Using a food processor or blender, puree, leaving the sauce slightly chunky, and return to pot. Or, use an immersion blender and puree directly in the pot.

5. Turn heat up to medium-high and cook, uncovered, for 15 to 20 minutes, or until sauce reduces to about ½ of its original content.

Equipment

All you really need to make great pizza dough products at home are a bowl for mixing, a wooden spoon, a large, flat surface for kneading and rolling (a clean countertop works splendidly), a regular old baking sheet, and a sharp knife. That said, I can suggest a few gadgets to make it easier, faster, and better tasting. While they are by no means required, they are fun.

Dough docker. A handy tool that most professional pizzerias use is a dough docker. Resembling a miniature rolling pin with pointed spikes on the roller, dough dockers place small dimples in the raw pizza dough and help minimize the amount of bubbling. Using a docker will assure that your homemade pizza does not come out all swollen and possibly burned in places.

Pizza cutter. Once the pizza or calzone is baked, you will need something to cut it into individual slices. Several different pizza cutters are available, and though a good, sharp knife will always get the job done, most seasoned pizza chefs opt for the traditional pizza cutter wheel. Look for a sturdy, very sharp one, ideally with a wooden handle and an easy grip.

Pizza pan. The most common method for baking pizza is with a pizza pan. Some pizzas, like thick crust or deep dish, require the use of a special pan because those pizzas will not hold together otherwise. Flat, solid pans are convenient because they also double as a serving tray. For thin-crust pizzas, piadinas, calzones, or flatbreads though, a regular baking sheet yields the same results.

Pizza peel. Pizza peels look like giant wooden spatulas and provide a preparation surface that makes for an easy transfer of uncooked pizza dough into the oven. Before placing the pizza dough on the peel, you will want to lightly dust it with either flour or cornmeal, so the pizza will easily slide off the peel into the oven. Choose a peel with a shorter handle (the big ones are for giant commercial ovens), so that it is easier to manipulate in the kitchen.

Pizza screen. Cheaper than a pizza stone, but also quite effective in delivering restaurant-quality pizza, is a pizza screen, which looks like a pizza pan with tiny holes in it. Pizza screens do two things: (1) they allow better heat transfer to the bottom of the pizza, so the pizza will bake faster, and (2) they also help yield a crispier crust, since all those little holes fight sogginess.

Pizza stone. While a backyard wood-fired brick oven will give you truly authentic, restaurant-style pizza, it will also cost you thousands of dollars to put in. A marble pizza stone, however, will make a close approximation in your home oven. Simply preheat the stone in your oven, place the pizza (or calzone, or piadina, or pretzel, etc.) directly on the stone once it is hot, and bake as directed. The pizza stone will deliver the same kind of char and flavoring as a wood-fired brick oven—for a tiny fraction of the price (most pizza stones cost $20 to $40).

Standing mixer. A standing mixer (the most common brand is KitchenAid) can make your dough stirring and kneading an absolute snap. Simply combine the ingredients in the bowl, turn on the paddle to stir, and then switch to the dough hook to knead. It makes the whole thing quite easy and quick.

CHAPTER 1

DOUGH

In case you haven't realized it yet, this book is about pizza dough. It is the foundation of all the recipes I've included here, and I am confident that pretty soon it will become the backbone of your cooking.

But first, a word about the Fear of Dough.

Are you afraid of dough?

It's okay; you can tell me.

If you are, you're not alone. Many people (some of them my friends and family) maintain the belief that they, despite their obvious innate intelligence, cannot handle making homemade dough. They hold deep-seated (though totally irrational and unsubstantiated) beliefs that making homemade dough requires a masters degree, a doctorate, a black belt, and the ability to perform magic.

Well I'm here to gently, lovingly inform you that if you managed to stir paste in kindergarten, you can make fresh pizza dough—it's that easy. You can make a little and use it right away, or you can make a lot and freeze some. You can flavor it with different herbs, spices and add-ins. You can even make it gluten free.

But before we get too crazy, let's start with some basics.

Using Store-bought Dough

Many grocery stores sell bagged, refrigerated pizza dough. While I truly believe homemade dough is always the most delicious option, store-bought can be a great time-saver when you're in a rush or just don't feel like getting out the flour.

When working with store-bought dough, there are a few tips and tricks to adhere to:

- Always let the dough come to room temperature before you begin shaping it. This will make it much more responsive to your touch, and it will be easier to work with. I like to do this by putting it in an oiled bowl, covering it with a clean dish towel, and placing it in a warm place, like an oven that has been pre-heated and then turned off (so it's warm, not hot), and leaving it alone for 20 or 30 minutes, while I prepare my other ingredients.

- Don't knead the dough beyond rolling or shaping into whatever you're making. It's already been kneaded and risen, and doing more to it will over-develop the gluten, making it tough and hard to work with.

- Stay away from canned doughs. They tend to have a funny aftertaste and often contain preservatives.

Fresh pizza dough also can be easily frozen, and if stored properly, it will keep for up to 3 months.

Freezing Pizza Dough

I almost always make a double batch of pizza dough and freeze half, so I'm never caught without. Plus, it means I get twice the product for half the amount of work, and that's always a good thing.

To freeze pizza dough:

1. Gather your finished (kneaded, risen) dough into a ball.

2. Gently coat the dough ball with olive or vegetable oil.

3. Slide the dough ball into a freezer-safe zip-top bag and seal, making sure to squeeze out the air.

4. Store in the freezer and freeze for up to 3 months.

5. When ready to use the dough, place in the fridge overnight (for about 12 hours) or thaw on a counter-top for 6 to 8 hours.

6. If you thawed your pizza dough in the refrigerator, allow it to come to room temperature, covered, in an oiled bowl for 20 to 30 minutes before using.

Basic Pizza Dough

This is the holy grail. You can make every recipe in this book with this dough, and it serves as the foundation of much of what goes on in my kitchen. I make it at least once a week.

1 cup warm water (110°F—or warm enough to take a comfortable shower)

1 packet active dry yeast

2 tablespoons sugar

1 teaspoon salt

2½ cups all-purpose flour

2 tablespoons olive oil, plus more for the bowl

1.Preheat the oven to 350°F, then turn it off as soon as it has preheated. This will allow the oven to be warm enough for when you make the dough.

2.Combine water, yeast, and sugar and set aside in a warm place until the mixture begins to foam, 4 to 5 minutes.

3. Meanwhile, in a mixing bowl, in a mixer with a paddle, or in a food processor, combine salt and flour. Slowly stream in the yeast mixture and add the olive oil. If using a mixer or food processor, turn on the machine and allow ingredients to combine until they form a ball of dough. If you're using a mixer, now is the time to switch to the dough hook. Knead (either by turning on your machine or by hand) for 2 to 3 minutes. If you're working by hand, continue stirring until a ball of dough forms.

4. Set dough aside to rise in an oiled bowl, covered with a damp dish towel in the warmed oven for 30 minutes.

5. Punch the dough down, let rest for 5 to 10 minutes, and then use as is. Alternately, make one of the variations (see page 21).

6. Prepare the dough as indicated in the recipe of your choice.

Herb-Garlic Pizza Dough

Make the basic pizza dough as instructed on page 19 but stir in 2 minced garlic cloves and 1 tablespoon each chopped fresh oregano and basil.

Rye Pizza Dough

Prepare basic pizza dough as directed on page 19 but substitute 1 cup of dark rye flour for 1 cup of the all-purpose flour.

Chocolate Pizza Dough

Make basic pizza dough as directed on page 19 but stir 1 cup of dark cocoa powder into the dry ingredients and use an extra ½ cup of water.

Pumpkin Pizza Dough

This orange dough is given a fiber and vitamin C boost from canned, pureed pumpkin. Following the basic recipe on page 19, simply increase the flour to 3 cups and add ½ cup canned, pureed unsweetened pumpkin.

Honey Whole-Wheat Pizza Dough

Following the basic recipe on page 19, use honey instead of sugar to activate the yeast and replace half of the all-purpose flour with whole-wheat flour.

PREP TIME: 3 hours
(not including starter)
TOTAL TIME: 3 hours
YIELD: 1 pound pizza dough

Sourdough Pizza Dough

This outrageously tasty, deeply flavorful dough variety takes a bit of extra time, but it's well worth it. You can find sourdough starter at most well-stocked grocery stores or gourmet grocers, or you can make it yourself with this recipe.

STARTER

3 cups warm water, plus more as needed

1 tablespoon honey or sugar

1 packet active dry yeast

4 cups all-purpose flour, plus more as needed

DOUGH

1 cup sourdough starter

½ cup hot (120°F) tap water

2½ cups all-purpose flour

1 teaspoon salt

1 packet active dry yeast

1. TO PREPARE THE STARTER: In a large glass bowl, pour 2 cups warm (110° F) water. Dissolve 1 tablespoon of honey or sugar in the water, then add the active dry yeast, and stir gently to dissolve. Gradually stir in 2 cups of the flour, and then cover the bowl with a clean dish cloth. The mixture will begin to bubble almost immediately.

2. Place the bowl in a warm place and let it sit for 8 to 12 hours. After the 8 to 12 hours, stir the sourdough starter and discard half. Add ½ cup warm water and another cup of flour. The starter mixture should have the consistency of thick pancake batter. Cover the bowl with the towel again and let sit for 2 to 4 hours more, until bubbly again.

3. After the 2 to 4 hours, stir the starter and discard half again. Add another ½ cup warm water and 1 cup flour. Cover the bowl with the dish cloth again and let sit 2 to 4 hours longer. The starter should be bubbly, though not as bubbly as it was when you first started.

4. Stir the starter down and then place it in a glass container (I keep mine in a large mason jar), loosely covered with a lid. Store in the refrigerator. Every week or so, discard half of it, and then stir in ½ cup warm water and a cup of flour. If you continue doing this, it will live indefinitely!

5. **TO MAKE THE DOUGH:** Stir any liquid that may have separated into the sourdough starter and spoon 1 cup of the starter into a mixing bowl.

6. Add the hot water, flour, salt, and yeast. Mix to combine and then knead until smooth and slightly sticky, about 10 minutes by hand on a floured surface, or 7 minutes at medium speed using a stand mixer with a dough hook.

7. Place the kneaded dough in a lightly oiled bowl and allow it to rise until it's just about doubled in size, about 2 hours.

8. Punch the dough down, let rest for 10 minutes, and then use as needed.

9. Prepare the dough as indicated in the recipe of your choice.

PREP TIME: 2 hours (including rising)
TOTAL TIME: 2 hours, 35 minutes
YIELD: 1 pound pizza dough

Egg Pizza Dough

Based on the style of challah and brioche, this dough is richened with egg and additional oil. It's soft and creamy on the inside with a very pleasant, chewy exterior. I use it to make pizzas with subtle flavors, like truffle oil, mushrooms, and rich cheeses.

¼ cup warm (about 110°F) water

½ cup extra-virgin olive or vegetable/canola oil, plus more for the bowl

1 packet active dry yeast

⅓ cup plus 2 tablespoons sugar

2 eggs, lightly beaten

1 teaspoon salt

4 cups all-purpose flour, plus more for kneading

1. Preheat the oven to 350°F and then turn it off, creating a warm (but not hot) place for the dough to rise.

2. In a mixing bowl, combine the warm water and olive oil. Add the yeast and 2 tablespoons of the sugar and stir gently. Let activate until it begins to foam slightly, 4 to 5 minutes.

3. Add the eggs, remaining sugar, salt, and flour and stir to combine. You should have a very soft dough.

4. Turn the dough out onto a floured surface and knead for about 10 minutes, until the dough is very elastic. (This can also be done in a stand-up mixer.) Roll the kneaded dough into a large ball.

5. Drizzle about 2 tablespoons of oil into a large bowl and place the dough in it. Turn the dough over in the bowl to make sure it's completely covered with oil.

6. Cover the bowl with a dish towel, and then put in the warm oven for 45 minutes to an hour, or until dough has increased by about two-thirds in size.

7. Prepare the dough as indicated in the recipe of your choice.

Gluten-Free Pizza Dough

More and more people are cutting gluten out of their diets these days. Pizza lovers need not worry. This gluten-free dough is a cinch to make and delicious!

1 packet active dry yeast

¼ cup warm (about 110°F) water, plus more as needed

2 teaspoons sugar or honey

1½ cups gluten-free all-purpose flour (My favorite is the Gluten-Free Pantry Flour from Glutino. It's also the cheapest available.)

2 tablespoons whole psyllium husks (available in the supplement aisle of most grocers)

1 teaspoon salt

¼ cup extra-virgin olive oil, plus more for brushing

1. Combine the yeast, water, and sugar in a small bowl. Stir gently and then let the mixture sit until it activates, 2 to 3 minutes.

2. Combine the flour, psyllium husks, and salt in a mixing bowl or the bowl of a stand-up mixer. Gently stir in the olive oil and the yeast mixture. You may need to add more warm water, a little bit at a time, until a soft, somewhat sticky dough forms.

3. Gather the dough into a ball and then put it back in its mixing bowl. Cover with a clean dish towel and let rise for an hour. (The dough won't increase in size much, but the flavor will develop immensely and the texture will improve.)

4. Prepare the dough as indicated in the recipe of your choice.

Notes: *After weeks of recipe testing and experimentation, here is what I learned:*

· *Gluten-free dough neither behaves nor tastes exactly like regular wheat dough. It's not going to be kneadable, rise in the same way, or stretch, and therefore it can't be used in every non-pizza recipe in this book.*

· *Prebaking is your friend. Prebaking a gluten-free crust means you can load it up with extra toppings without worrying about it getting soggy.*

· *It's all about the olive oil. Gluten-free doughs can dry out easily. Counteract that tendency with a liberal brushing of delicious olive oil. It'll add flavor and moisture at the same time.*

CHAPTER 2

SNACKS
AND
APPETIZERS

The secret to throwing a good cocktail party is stellar appetizers. And can you guess what the secret to stellar appetizers is? Yep, you guessed it. Pizza dough. Think of pizza dough as a canvas for your creativity—a canvas far beyond pizza itself. Anything you might do with pie dough or puff pastry can be done with pizza dough, yielding a different but totally yummy result.

   All of the pockets and pinwheels in this section freeze very well, so you might consider making a double batch and freezing half to have on hand to bake as needed. They make great, kid-friendly snacks, or even a light grown-up dinner.

Artichoke Pocket Squares

What's better than hot, bubbly artichoke dip? How about these totally portable (and much easier to eat) pizza pockets? Creamy, Parmesan-laced artichoke dip is rolled up tightly in your choice of dough.

Flour for baking sheet and rolling

6 ounces canned artichoke hearts, drained and chopped

1½ cups freshly grated Parmesan

⅔ cup mayonnaise

½ teaspoon each salt and freshly ground black pepper

1 handful fresh flat-leaf parsley, finely chopped

1 recipe pizza dough

RECOMMENDED DOUGHS: *Basic, Herb-Garlic, Sourdough*

1. Preheat the oven to 375°F. Lightly flour a baking sheet and set aside.

2. In a bowl, stir artichokes together with the Parmesan, mayonnaise, salt, pepper, and parsley and then set aside.

3. On a lightly floured surface, roll the pizza dough out into a large rectangle, about 14-by-10 inches. Cut the rectangle in half and set one half aside on a floured surface.

4. Drop tablespoon-size dollops of the artichoke dip over one sheet of dough, with about an inch between each dollop. Use a pastry brush to brush a small amount of water around each dollop and then top with the second sheet of dough, pressing around each dollop to seal, as if making ravioli.

5. Use a sharp knife to cut out little pockets and transfer them to the prepared baking sheet. If scraps remain, re-roll and repeat the process.

6. Bake the pockets for 12 to 15 minutes, or until golden brown and crispy.

Gorgonzola-Pear Pocket Squares

Sweet, juicy pear dances with creamy, assertive Gorgonzola in an elegant, attractive little pocket. Like the artichoke dip pockets (on the facing page), this is a quick way to make a fancy appetizer for a whole lot less effort than you'd think.

These sweet, savory, and decidedly grown-up pockets are perfect served in the sunshine with a flute of crisp Prosecco or Champagne.

Flour for baking sheet and rolling

3 ripe Bosc or Anjou pears, cored and chopped into ½-inch pieces

½ cup crumbled Gorgonzola

1 cup (8 ounces) cream cheese, at room temperature

1 teaspoon freshly ground black pepper

Salt

¼ cup toasted pecans, chopped (see note)

1 recipe pizza dough

RECOMMENDED DOUGHS: *Basic, Egg*

1. Preheat the oven to 375°F. Lightly flour a baking sheet and set aside.

2. Combine the chopped pears, toasted pecans, Gorgonzola, cream cheese, pepper, and salt to taste. Stir well to combine.

3. On a lightly floured surface, roll the pizza dough out into a large rectangle, about 14-by-10 inches. Cut the dough in half and set one half aside on a floured surface.

4. Drop tablespoon-size dollops of the Gorgonzola mixture over one sheet of dough, with about an inch between each dollop. Use a pastry brush to brush a small amount of water around each dollop and then top with the second sheet of dough, pressing around each dollop to seal, as if making ravioli.

5. Use a sharp knife to cut out little pockets and transfer them to a baking sheet. If scraps remain, re-roll and repeat the process.

6. Bake the pockets for 12 to 15 minutes, or until golden brown and crispy.

Note: *To toast nuts, spread on a rimmed baking sheet and bake in a preheated 350°F oven, stirring occasionally, until fragrant, about 10 minutes. Let cool completely.*

Ham and Cheese Pocket Moons

These unassuming little half-moons are like hot ham and cheese sandwiches, in a neat, tidy, and easy-to-eat package. They're kid-friendly, and great for parties, sports events, or even a quick dinner.

Flour for baking sheet and rolling

6 ounces chopped Black Forest ham

½ cup (4 ounces) cream cheese, at room temperature

1 cup shredded sharp cheddar cheese

½ teaspoon freshly ground black pepper

1 recipe pizza dough

Extra-virgin olive oil for brushing

RECOMMENDED DOUGHS: *Basic, Sourdough, Egg*

1. Preheat the oven to 450°F. Lightly flour a baking sheet and set aside.

2. In a mixing bowl, combine the ham, cream cheese, cheddar cheese, and black pepper. Stir well to combine and set aside.

3. On a lightly floured surface, use a rolling pin to roll the dough out until it is about ⅛ inch thick. Use a small bowl, large glass, or cookie cutter to cut the dough into eight 4-inch circles (feel free to go slightly larger or smaller).

4. Place 2 tablespoons of the ham-and-cheese mixture in the center of each of the circles. Fold the dough rounds in half to form a little half-moon. Tuck the ends from underneath the bottom half of the dough over the top half and pinch gently to seal.

5. Arrange the pockets on the prepared baking sheet and brush lightly with olive oil. Bake until golden brown, 12 to 14 minutes. (Don't worry if a little filling seeps out while baking.) Serve warm.

Hint: *Make a double batch of the pockets and freeze half of them on parchment paper, unbaked. Store in a zip-top bag, and bake, straight out of the freezer when ready to use.*

Ricotta-Tomato Pocket Moons

"This is perfect bachelor food," my friend Josh said when I made these. "Simple ingredients, minimal technique, and maximum results. I would totally make this."

There you have it—straight from the bachelor's mouth.

Flour for baking sheet and rolling

1 cup (8 ounces) canned, crushed tomatoes

1 handful fresh basil, chopped

Salt and freshly ground black pepper

1 recipe pizza dough

8 tablespoons ricotta cheese (preferably whole milk)

4 ounces pepperoni, chopped (optional)

Extra-virgin olive oil for brushing

RECOMMENDED DOUGHS: *Basic, Herb-Garlic, Sourdough*

1. Preheat the oven to 450°F. Lightly flour a baking sheet and set aside.

2. In a small bowl, stir together the crushed tomatoes, the basil, salt, and pepper. Set aside.

3. On a lightly floured surface, use a rolling pin to roll the dough out until it is about ⅛ inch thick. Use a small bowl, large glass, or cookie cutter to cut the dough into eight 4-inch rounds. (Feel free to go slightly larger or smaller.)

4. Place a heaping tablespoon of the tomato sauce on one half of each of the rounds. Place 1 tablespoon of ricotta next to each spoonful of the sauce. Add a pinch of chopped pepperoni, if using.

5. Fold the dough rounds in half to form a little half-moon. Tuck the ends from underneath the bottom half of the dough over the top half and pinch gently to seal.

6. Arrange the calzones on the prepared baking sheet and brush lightly with olive oil. Bake until golden brown, 12 to 14 minutes. (Don't worry if a little filling seeps out while baking.) Serve warm.

Apple-Onion Tartlets with Cheddar

Sweetness from the caramelized onions and apples is contrasted with salty cheddar cheese and spicy black pepper. Make these for a light supper, served with a green salad.

Flour for baking sheet and rolling

2 tablespoons extra-virgin olive oil

2 medium onions, thinly sliced

½ teaspoon each salt and freshly ground black pepper

1 recipe pizza dough

2 Granny Smith apples, cored and thinly sliced

½ cup shredded cheddar cheese

RECOMMENDED DOUGHS: *Basic, Honey Whole-Wheat, Sourdough*

1. Preheat the oven to 400°F. Lightly flour a baking sheet and set aside.

2. Heat the oil in a large frying pan over medium-low heat. Add the onions and stir a few times to distribute the oil evenly. Add the salt and pepper and stir again. Cook for 18 to 20 minutes, allowing the onions to caramelize, stirring once or twice throughout cooking.

3. Meanwhile, divide the dough into 4 even balls on a lightly floured surface. Use your hands or a rolling pin to roll each ball out into a 6-inch round. Set the rounds on the prepared baking sheet. (It's okay if the dough circles touch; they won't when you're done assembling the tartlets.)

4. Arrange about half-an-apple's worth of slices in a circle in the center of one of the dough rounds. Make sure to leave a border of about 1½ inches of dough. Top the circle of apples with a quarter of the caramelized onions.

5. Fold in the border of dough to form a tartlet. (It's supposed to look rustic, so don't worry about making it look perfect.) Sprinkle the whole tartlet (crust included) with ⅛ cup cheddar cheese.

6. Repeat the tartlet-making process with the remaining ingredients to make 4 tartlets.

7. Bake until the crusts are golden brown and the cheese is bubbly, 18 to 22 minutes. Serve the tartlets whole or cut into wedges.

Tomato-Feta Tartlets

Like the Apple-Onion Tartlets with Cheddar (page 35), these little pies are as pretty to look at as they are to eat. Serve a whole tartlet to each person or cut each into wedges and tuck them into a basket to be passed at the table.

Flour for baking sheet and rolling

2 tablespoons extra-virgin olive oil

2 medium onions, thinly sliced

½ teaspoon each salt and freshly ground black pepper

1 recipe pizza dough

4 Roma tomatoes, sliced

½ cup crumbled feta cheese, plus more if desired

RECOMMENDED DOUGHS: *Basic, Herb-Garlic, Sourdough*

1. Preheat the oven to 400°F. Lightly flour a baking sheet and set aside.

2. Heat the oil in a large frying pan over medium-low heat. Add the onions and stir a few times to distribute the oil evenly. Add the salt and pepper and stir again. Cook for 18 to 20 minutes, allowing the onions to caramelize, stirring once or twice throughout cooking.

3. Meanwhile, divide the dough into 4 even balls on a lightly floured surface. Use your hands or a rolling pin to roll each ball out into a 6-inch round. Set the rounds on the prepared baking sheet. (It's okay if the dough circles touch; they won't when you're done assembling the tartlets.)

4. Arrange about a quarter of the caramelized onions in a circle in the center of one of the dough rounds. Make sure to leave a border of about 1½ inches of dough. Top the circle of onions with 1 tomato's worth of slices.

5. Fold in the border of dough to form a tartlet. (It's supposed to look rustic, so don't worry about making it look perfect.) Sprinkle the tartlet (crust included) with ⅛ cup feta cheese (or more to taste).

6. Repeat the tartlet-making process with the remaining ingredients to make 4 tartlets.

7. Bake until the crust is golden brown, 18 to 22 minutes.

Red Pepper–Goat Cheese Tartlets This flavor combination was inspired by an excellent bruschetta I had one afternoon at a tiny bed-and-breakfast in Bodega Bay, California. Soft creamy goat cheese was spread across pieces of crusty, toasted baguette and topped with roasted red peppers, fresh basil leaves, salt, and pepper. It was pure testament to the fact that simple, fresh ingredients yield delicious food. Here, I've baked the same lovely combination into little tarts—perfect with soup, salad, or just by themselves.

Flour for baking sheet and rolling

2 tablespoons extra-virgin olive oil

2 medium onions, thinly sliced

½ teaspoon each salt and freshly ground black pepper

1 recipe pizza dough

Two 8-ounce jars chopped roasted red peppers, drained

½ cup crumbled goat cheese

1 handful fresh basil leaves, thinly sliced

RECOMMENDED DOUGHS: *Basic, Herb-Garlic, Sourdough*

1. Preheat the oven to 400°F. Lightly flour a baking sheet and set aside.

2. Heat the oil in a large frying pan over medium-low heat. Add the onions and stir a few times to distribute the oil evenly. Add the salt and pepper and stir again. Cook for 18 to 20 minutes, allowing the onions to caramelize, stirring once or twice throughout cooking.

3. Meanwhile, divide the dough into 4 even balls on a lightly floured surface. Use your hands or a rolling pin to roll each ball out into a 6-inch round. Set the rounds on the prepared baking sheet. (It's okay if they touch; they won't when you're done assembling the tartlets.)

4. Arrange a quarter of the red peppers in a circle in the center of one of the dough rounds. Make sure to leave a border of about 1½ inches of dough. Top the circle of red peppers with about a quarter of the caramelized onions.

5. Fold in the border of dough to form a tartlet. (It's supposed to look rustic, so don't worry about making it look perfect.) Sprinkle the whole tartlet (crust included) with $\frac{1}{8}$ cup of the goat cheese.

6. Repeat the process with the remaining ingredients to make 4 tartlets.

7. Bake until the crust is crisp and the cheese is browned, 18 to 22 minutes. Top each tartlet with a sprinkling of fresh basil and serve whole or cut into wedges.

PREP TIME: 15 minutes
TOTAL TIME: 40 minutes
YIELD: 20 pinwheels (serves 8 to 10)

Cheesy Pizza Pinwheels

I also call these "picnic pizzas," because they are so portable and fun to eat on a blanket in the park. They're hypnotizingly flavorful, cheesy, crispy circles of deliciousness that lend themselves to many flavor combinations. Feel free to add your favorite pizza toppings before rolling up.

Flour for baking sheet and rolling

1 recipe pizza dough

1 cup sauce (see page 11)

1 cup shredded or crumbled cheese, such as mozarella, smoked mozarella or aged white cheddar.

1 to 2 cups toppings, such as sliced black olives, spinach, chopped pepperoni, or chopped mushrooms (optional)

Salt and freshly ground black pepper

1 egg

1 tablespoon water

RECOMMENDED DOUGHS: *Basic, Herb-Garlic, Honey Whole-Wheat, Sourdough*

1. Preheat the oven to 375°F. Lightly flour a baking sheet and set aside.

2. On a lightly floured surface, roll the pizza dough out into a large rectangle, about 14-by-10 inches and spread the dough with the desired sauce. Sprinkle the cheese and scatter the toppings over the sauced, cheesed dough (remember not to go too heavy). Top with a light sprinkling of salt and pepper. Roll the dough up the long way, pinching the edge as you go to ensure a tight seal. When you finish rolling the dough, you should have a 10-inch log.

3. Use a sharp knife to slice the log into twenty ½-inch-thick pieces. Lay each slice on the prepared baking sheet.

4. In a small bowl, beat the egg with the water. Then, using a pastry brush, lightly coat each pinwheel with the egg wash.

5. Bake until the crust is golden brown and the filling is bubbly, 18 to 22 minutes. Serve warm or at room temperature.

PREP TIME: 25 minutes
TOTAL TIME: 30 minutes
YIELD: 6 empanadas (serves 3 to 4)

Butternut Squash Empanadas

This festive fall-inspired version of the empanada is perfect for an autumn picnic. I like to pack them in foil packets, along with a hearty kale salad for an early evening dinner picnic.

Flour for baking sheet and rolling

2 cups diced (¼ inch) butternut squash from 1 medium-size squash

¼ cup extra-virgin olive oil

½ cup finely chopped white onion

6 small garlic cloves, minced

Two 2- to 3-inch fresh jalapeño chiles, seeds and ribs discarded and chiles finely chopped

½ teaspoon salt, plus more as desired

⅓ cup chicken broth

1 recipe pizza dough

1 egg

2 tablespoons water

1½ teaspoons sea salt for sprinkling (optional)

RECOMMENDED DOUGHS: *Basic, Pumpkin, Honey Whole-Wheat*

1. Lightly flour a large baking sheet and set aside.

2. Cook squash pieces in a small saucepan of boiling salted water until just tender, about 2 minutes. Drain and set aside.

3. Heat the oil in a large heavy-bottomed saucepan over medium-low heat. Add the onion and garlic, stirring until softened, about 3 minutes. Add the jalapeños and cook, stirring, 1 minute. Stir in salt and broth and simmer, covered, about 2 minutes. Simmer, uncovered, stirring occasionally, until the liquid is evaporated, about 3 minutes, then stir in the squash and salt to taste. Cool filling completely.

4. Divide the dough into 8 equal portions and form each into a disk. Roll out 1 piece on a lightly floured surface into a 6- to 7-inch round (about ⅛ inch thick).

5. In a small bowl, beat the egg with the water to make an egg wash. Set aside.

6. Spoon about ⅓ cup of the filling into the center of the dough and brush the edge of the dough lightly with egg wash. Fold the dough in half to form a half-moon, enclosing the filling, and press edges together to seal. Crimp the edge decoratively and use a spatula to transfer the empanada to the prepared sheet. Repeat the process to make a total of 6 empanadas.

7. Lightly brush empanadas all over with some of the remaining egg wash and sprinkle each with ¼ teaspoon sea salt, if using. Bake on center rack of the oven until golden, 25 to 30 minutes. Serve warm or at room temperature.

Bean and Cheese Empanadas

Empanadas are the calzones of South and Central America. Traditionally, the dough is made with butter or shortening, yielding a crisp, crumbly exterior, but in this instance, I opt for chewy-crisp pizza dough.

1 recipe pizza dough

Flour for rolling

1 sixteen-ounce can refried beans

1 one-pint container fresh salsa

1 cup shredded Jack cheese

2 tablespoons extra-virgin olive oil

1 egg

1 tablespoon water

Sour cream for serving (optional)

RECOMMENDED DOUGHS: *Basic, Pumpkin, Honey Whole-Wheat*

1. Preheat the oven to 400°F.

2. Divide the dough into 6 equal portions. Roll each into an 8-inch round on a lightly floured surface.

3. In a small bowl, beat the egg with the water to make an egg wash. Set aside.

4. On half of each round, spread some of the beans. Top each with 1½ tablespoons of the salsa and sprinkle each with 2 tablespoons of the cheese.

5. Fold over the other half of each round, covering the filling, and press the curved edge with your thumb to seal.

6. Spread 1 teaspoon of the oil on a baking sheet. Transfer the empanadas to the prepared sheet and lightly brush empanadas all over with the egg wash.

7. Bake until golden, 12 to 15 minutes. Serve with a dollop of sour cream, if desired.

PREP TIME: 40 minutes
TOTAL TIME: 1 hour, 10 minutes
YIELD: 14 to 16 pizzettas
(serves 3 to 4)

Pear-Goat Cheese Pizzettas

These elegant pizzettas can be served along with a simple soup or crisp green salad for a supper, or slice them thinly and serve with crisp Chardonnay or Prosecco. The pizzettas are great hot or at room temperature.

2 tablespoons extra-virgin olive oil

1 large sweet onion, sliced

1 medium-ripe pear, sliced

2 tablespoons balsamic vinegar

½ teaspoon freshly ground black pepper

1 recipe pizza dough

Flour for rolling

½ cup crumbled goat cheese

¼ cup chopped walnuts

RECOMMENDED DOUGHS: *Basic, Honey Whole-Wheat, Sourdough, Egg*

1. Preheat the oven to 450°F.

2. Heat 1 tablespoon of the oil in a large nonstick skillet over medium-high heat. Add the onion and cook, stirring often, until soft and golden, about 7 minutes. Stir in the pear slices and cook, stirring often, until slightly soft and heated through, 1 to 2 minutes. Add the vinegar and pepper and continue cooking, stirring often, until the liquid has evaporated and the onion is tender and coated with a dark glaze, about 2 minutes more.

3. Divide the dough into 6 equal portions. Roll each into an 8-inch round on a lightly floured surface.

4. Divide the onion-pear mixture among the dough rounds; sprinkle with cheese and walnuts.

5. Spread the remaining 1 tablespoon oil on a large baking sheet.

6. Transfer the pizzettas to the prepared sheet and bake until crispy and the cheese is melted, 10 to 15 minutes. Serve at once.

PREP TIME: 25 minutes
TOTAL TIME: 40 minutes
YIELD: 14 to 16 pizza rolls
(serves 4 to 6)

Homemade Pizza Rolls

I'll be honest: I don't care about football. I am a gatherer, not a hunter. So when I watch football, I get confused and then bored trying to keep track of objects flying through the air and men jumping on top of each other, all within increments of time that don't match up to what is actually on the clock. I am forever accidentally referring to my brother's fantasy football team as his "imaginary football team" and have even been known to ask, "What inning is this?"

But football has a bigger association for me—pizza rolls. As a kid, I admit to enjoying the Totino's frozen variety and eventually switching to the organic Amy's Kitchen kind. But now I try to avoid frozen convenience food at all costs, so I figured I'd try making them myself. Turns out it's ridiculously easy, so read on.

Go Niners! Or Packers? Steelers? Or whatever. Pass the pizza rolls.

Oil for baking sheet

One 15-ounce can crushed tomatoes

1 teaspoon dried basil

⅔ cup shredded mozzarella cheese

2 cloves garlic, finely minced

Salt and freshly ground black pepper

1 recipe pizza dough

Flour for rolling

1 egg

1 tablespoon water

RECOMMENDED DOUGHS: *Basic, Herb-Garlic, Honey Whole-Wheat, Sourdough*

1. Preheat the oven to 400°F. Lightly oil a baking sheet and set aside.

2. In a mixing bowl, combine the crushed tomatoes, basil, mozzarella, and garlic. Add salt and pepper to taste. Stir well.

3. Roll the dough out on a lightly floured surface until it is about ⅛ inch thick. Use a floured 4-inch cookie cutter, cup, or bowl (I used a plastic food container, which worked well) to cut the dough into rounds. Re-roll scraps and continue cutting until all dough has been used up. You should have 14 to 16 rounds.

4. Place about 1½ tablespoons of the tomato filling on one half of each dough round. Fold the other half over and press gently (but firmly) along the edges of the circle to seal it, forming a half-moon. Use the back of a fork to create a scalloped edge along the seal. Transfer the roll to the prepared baking sheet. Repeat with the remaining dough rounds.

5. Beat the egg with the water to make an egg wash. Brush the tops of the pizza rolls with the egg wash.

6. Bake the pizza rolls for 12 to 15 minutes, or until golden brown, and serve hot.

Honey Whole-Wheat Pretzels

Top these healthy, kid-friendly pretzels with anything you can dream up. I love using sesame and pumpkin seeds, fennel, and sea salt.

Oil for baking sheet

1 recipe pizza dough

1 tablespoon baking soda

1 egg, beaten

2 tablespoons large-grain salt, such as sea salt or rock salt (optional)

Mustard for dipping (optional)

RECOMMENDED DOUGH: *Honey Whole-Wheat*

1. Preheat the oven to 450°F. Lightly oil a baking sheet and set aside.

2. Fill a large pot with 10 cups of water. Place on the stove over high heat and whisk in the baking soda. Bring water to a boil.

3. Meanwhile, roll the dough out into ten 12-inch ropes and fold each rope into a pretzel shape (or other desired shape; see Note).

4. One at a time, drop each pretzel-shaped piece of dough into the water, boil for 5 seconds, and then transfer to the prepared baking sheet.

5. Use a pastry brush to lightly brush egg onto the pretzels. Sprinkle with salt or other toppings if desired. Bake until pretzels are golden brown, 12 to 15 minutes. Serve plain or with mustard for dipping.

Note: *To roll a pretzel shape, draw the ends of the rope together to form a circle. Twist the ends together once or twice. Layer the twisted ends onto the bottom curve of the shape. You can use a little water to wet the ends to make them stick.*

PREP TIME: 25 minutes
TOTAL TIME: 1 hour, 15 minutes
YIELD: 8 knishes (serves 2 to 4)

Potato-Cheddar Knishes

I was first introduced to knishes at Zaftig's, where my friend Ryan and I would nurse hangovers on weekend mornings during college. These puffy, flaky knishes have all the healing power of chicken noodle soup; they make you feel warm and loved.

Flour for baking sheet and rolling

2 large russet potatoes, scrubbed and diced with peels intact

2 tablespoons unsalted butter

1 small onion, diced

½ teaspoon (about 2 twigs) fresh thyme

⅓ cup shredded sharp cheddar cheese

Salt and freshly ground black pepper

1 recipe pizza dough

1 egg

1 tablespoon water

Sour cream (optional)

RECOMMENDED DOUGHS: *Basic, Egg*

1. Preheat the oven to 375°F. Lightly dust a baking sheet with flour and set aside.

2. Bring a pot of salted water to a boil. Add the diced potatoes and cook until very soft, 12 to 15 minutes. While potatoes cook, heat the butter in a medium frying pan over medium-high heat. Add the onion and thyme and cook for 5 to 6 minutes, until onions are lightly browned and very fragrant. Remove from heat and scrape into a mixing bowl. Once potatoes have cooked, drain them and add them to the bowl with the onions and thyme. Add the cheese and mash with a fork or potato masher until potatoes have very few lumps. Add ½ teaspoon salt and pepper to taste and set aside.

3. Knead the dough a few times and form it into a cylinder, about 8 inches long. Cut dough into 8 equal pieces. Use a rolling pin to roll each piece into a 4- to 5-inch round. Scoop 3 to 4 tablespoon of the potato mixture into the center of each round and pinch the ends together, to make a little bundle.

4. In a small bowl, beat the egg with the water. Use a pastry brush to lightly brush the tops of the knishes with the egg wash.

5. Bake until the knishes are golden brown, 15 to 18 minutes. Serve hot, with sour cream if desired.

PREP TIME: 10 minutes
TOTAL TIME: 25 minutes
YIELD: Six 8-inch flatbreads
(serves 3 to 6)

Chive Flatbread

This is one of my favorite accompaniments for soups or salads—turning them from side dish into full and special meal.

½ recipe pizza dough

Flour for rolling

1 small bunch chives, snipped into ¼-inch pieces

Extra-virgin olive oil

Salt

RECOMMENDED DOUGHS: *Basic, Honey Whole-Wheat*

1. Divide the dough into 6 pieces. On a clean, floured surface, roll the dough out into 6-inch rounds. Sprinkle some chives on a round and then use a rolling pin to press them into the dough. Repeat with the remaining dough.

2. Heat 2 teaspoons olive oil in a large frying pan over high heat. Fry the pieces of chive-rolled dough for 1 to 2 minutes on each side until brown and bubbly, adding more oil as needed. Sprinkle the flatbreads lightly with salt, cut into wedges, and serve.

PREP TIME: 25 minutes
TOTAL TIME: 40 minutes
YIELD: 2 flatbreads (serves 6 to 8)

Flatbread with Crème Fraiche, Smoked Salmon, and Dill

This unique flatbread features all the flavors of the classic lox-and-rye combination but in a much prettier presentation. I like to serve it as part of a spread, with scrambled eggs and fresh fruit.

Flour for baking sheet and rolling

1 recipe pizza dough, divided into 2 balls

Olive oil for brushing

6 ounces smoked salmon (lox)

One 4-ounce container crème fraiche or full-fat sour cream

Freshly ground black pepper

Few sprigs fresh dill

Sliced lemon for garnish (optional)

RECOMMENDED DOUGHS: *Basic, Rye, Honey Whole-Wheat, Sourdough*

1. Preheat the oven to 400°F. Lightly flour a baking sheet and set aside.

2. On another floured surface, roll each dough round out into an oblong shape, about 12 inches long. Set the dough pieces on the prepared baking sheet and, using a pastry brush, lightly brush the dough pieces with olive oil.

3. Bake until golden brown, 12 to 14 minutes. Let cool to room temperature.

4. Arrange the salmon attractively over the flatbreads. Using a spoon, drizzle the crème fraiche over the salmon. Top with black pepper and fresh dill sprigs. Slice into strips and serve, garnished with lemon slices, if desired.

CHAPTER 3

BREADS

One of the most wonderful things about pizza dough is that, if you can make it, you can make fresh bread—stat. Pizza is, after all, a very thin kind of bread anyway, right?

Once I figured this out, I started to realize the endless options for pizza dough. From simple breadsticks to home-made dinner rolls—even homemade bagels (!), it all came down to that one simple dough.

Once you start to master fresh breads, you'll learn the joy of a homemade sandwich on homemade bread. In this chapter, I've offered up some of my favorite combinations, but don't hesitate to try your favorite sandwich concoctions. It'll change your whole world view. . . not to mention, your lunch.

PREP TIME: 15 minutes
TOTAL TIME: 45 minutes
YIELD: 8 bagels (serves 8)

Bagels

These do-it-yourself bagels beat out the bagged, store-bought kind any day. If you've ever been to Montreal, you are no doubt familiar with the city's famous bagel style: smaller, slightly sweet bagels. To emulate it at home, simply roll your bagels slightly smaller (you'll end up with 8 or 9, as opposed to 6) and add a tablespoon or two of honey to your boiling water. Bake until toasty.

1 tablespoon vegetable oil for baking sheet

Flour for rolling

1 recipe pizza dough

½ cup sesame or poppy seeds

Kosher salt

RECOMMENDED DOUGHS: *Basic, Honey Whole-Wheat, Egg*

1. Preheat the oven to 400°F. Grease a large baking sheet with the vegetable oil.

2. Fill a large pot with water and bring it to a boil over high heat.

3. Meanwhile, prepare a floured surface for the dough. Cut the dough into 8 equal-sized pieces. Roll each piece into a 6-inch rope and connect the ends of the ropes to make 8 smallish bagels.

4. Carefully boil the bagels 2 or 3 at a time for about a minute each, or until they float. Transfer to a clean plate.

5. Spread the sesame seeds on another dry plate. One at a time, dip the bagels into the sesame seeds so the rounded top is covered with seeds. Sprinkle the other side lightly with Kosher salt.

6. Transfer all of the bagels to the prepared baking sheet. Bake until the bagels are golden brown, 10 to 15 minutes. Carefully turn bagels over and bake for an additional 5 minutes. Slice if desired and serve warm.

Bagels with Lox-Scallion Cream Cheese

This recipe is delicious using either smoked salmon or trout. In a food processor, combine fish, scallions, cream cheese, capers, salt, and freshly ground black pepper. Blend to whip. Serve on toasted bagels with tomato slices.

PREP TIME: 20 minutes
TOTAL TIME: 54 minutes
YIELD: 8 to 10 bialys (serves 4 to 5)

Bialys

No joke: my grandparents used to import bialys from New York. They would freeze them and store them in zip-top bags in the freezer of their Los Angeles kitchen. One of my favorite childhood memories is of sitting at their kitchen table, eating a hot, toasty bialy and sneaking sips of my grandfather's coffee.

Flour for baking sheet and rolling

1 recipe pizza dough

2 tablespoons olive oil or canola oil

½ onion, finely chopped

3 tablespoons poppy seeds

Salt and freshly ground black pepper

1 egg

1 tablespoon water

Butter or cream cheese (optional)

RECOMMENDED DOUGHS: *Basic, Sourdough*

1. Preheat the oven to 475°F. Lightly flour a baking sheet and set aside.

2. Cut the dough into 8 (for larger bialys) or 10 (for smaller ones) equal pieces. Shape each piece of dough into some semblance of a 4- or 5-inch round. Let the dough rounds rest for 10 to 15 minutes.

3. Meanwhile, heat the oil in a large frying pan over medium heat. Add the chopped onion and cook for 7 to 9 minutes, or until very soft and golden-brown. Add the poppy seeds and season with salt and pepper. Remove from heat and allow to cool slightly.

4. Beat the egg with the water to make an egg wash. Use a pastry brush to brush the dough rounds lightly with the egg wash. Then, using your thumb, create a small well in the center of each dough round. Put about 1 tablespoon of the onion mixture (more, if it will fit) into the well you created.

5. Place the bialys 1 to 2 inches apart on the prepared baking sheet. Bake until the bialys are golden brown, 12 to 14 minutes. Serve hot with butter or cream cheese—or just plain.

Bialys with Smoked Whitefish Salad

Top fresh bialys with lettuce, store-bought whitefish salad (look for it in the deli section), tomatoes, and capers. Finish with a few grinds of fresh black pepper and serve.

Italian Balloon Bread

This dramatic Italian bread, a variation of focaccia, is often found in trattorias across Italy. Nothing more than a tiny ball of pizza dough, it puffs up when baked and impresses everyone at the table. I first learned about it from Judy Zeidler's wonderful unpretentious cookbook *Italy Cooks* (Mostarda Press, 2011). It can be served simply with olive oil and salt, or spread with fresh ricotta.

Oil for baking sheet (optional)

Flour for rolling

½ recipe pizza dough

Extra-virgin olive oil

Salt

RECOMMENDED DOUGH: *Basic*

1. Remove all but one rack from your oven and move that rack to the lowest position in the oven. Heat the oven to 450°F and place a pizza stone or greased baking sheet inside on the rack you positioned.

2. Cut the dough into 4 equal pieces.

3. Place the dough pieces on a floured board, and press them into flat rounds with your palms. Using a rolling pin, roll out each piece of dough into an 8-inch round, ⅛ to ¼ inch thick.

4. Place one dough round on the stone or prepared baking sheet and bake until it puffs and is well browned, about 8 minutes. (Repeat with the remaining pieces of dough.) Do not open the oven door during the first 3 or 4 minutes.

5. Remove the breads from the oven, drizzle them with olive oil, sprinkle with salt, and serve warm.

PREP TIME: 10 minutes
TOTAL TIME: 30 minutes
YIELD: 6 to 8 breadsticks
(serves 3 to 4)

Cheesy Breadsticks with Tomato Sauce

Inspired by my hometown pizzeria's delicious solution to excess pizza dough, I serve these extremely kid-friendly breadsticks with tomato sauce for dipping, but they would also be right at home alongside salads or soups, or as the starch portion of a meal.

Flour for baking sheet and rolling

½ recipe pizza dough

Extra-virgin olive oil

½ cup shredded mozzarella or provolone cheese

Tomato sauce for dipping

RECOMMENDED DOUGHS: *Basic, Herb-Garlic, Sourdough*

1. Preheat the oven to 400°F. Lightly flour a baking sheet and set aside.

2. On another lightly floured surface, divide the dough into 6 to 8 equal pieces. Roll each piece of dough into a 6- to 7-inch snake shape.

3. Arrange the dough snakes on the prepared baking sheet and brush lightly with olive oil. Top each snake with a few pinches of cheese and bake until the cheese is golden brown and bubbly, 14 to 16 minutes. Serve warm, with the tomato sauce alongside.

PREP TIME: 10 minutes
TOTAL TIME: 30 minutes
YIELD: 6 to 8 breadsticks
(serves 3 to 4)

Twisted Garlic-Herb Breadsticks

These are a delicious twist (literally—ha!) on the Cheesy Breadsticks on page 59. Feel free to switch up the herbs. I love to use fresh basil, thyme, or rosemary, depending on what I'm serving them with.

Flour for baking sheet and rolling

½ recipe pizza dough

2 tablespoons extra-virgin olive oil

3 cloves garlic, minced

1 handful fresh parsley, minced

Salt

RECOMMENDED DOUGHS: *Herb-Garlic, Sourdough*

1. Preheat the oven to 400°F. Lightly flour a baking sheet and set aside.

2. On a lightly floured surface, divide the dough into 6 to 8 equal pieces. Roll each piece of dough into a 6- to 7-inch snake shape.

3. Stir the olive oil together with the garlic and parsley.

4. Arrange the dough snakes on the prepared baking sheet and brush lightly with the olive oil mixture. Gently twist each snake a few times. Sprinkle lightly with salt. Bake until golden brown, 14 to 16 minutes.

PREP TIME: 45 minutes
TOTAL TIME: 1 hour, 20 minutes
YIELD: Four 14-inch baguettes
(serves 8)

Quick Baguettes

Turn your kitchen into a French bakery in no time! These easy and very pretty baguettes elevate a regular old weeknight dinner into a romantic bistro-esque experience. Just add a pretty tablecloth and a bottle of wine.

Flour for baking sheet and rolling

I recipe pizza dough

RECOMMENDED DOUGHS: *Basic, Honey Whole-Wheat, Sourdough*

1. Preheat the oven to 450°F. Lightly flour a baking sheet and set aside.

2. Before shaping: Prepare the dough and let it rise as normal. When ready to shape the loaves, sprinkle your work surface generously with flour. Turn the dough out onto the floured surface and use a sharp knife to divide the dough into four equal pieces. Cover with plastic wrap and let the dough rest for about 15 minutes.

3. Sprinkle your work surface and one of the pieces of dough with more flour. Pat the dough into a rough rectangle, approximately 8-by-10 inches. Fold down the top third of the dough and use the heel of your hand to seal the edge.

4. Fold the bottom third of the dough up and use the heel of your hand to smooth out the edge. Use the edge of your hand to pat a crease in the middle of the dough and then fold in half again. This will create a taut and smooth surface to the dough. Seal the edges until smooth.

5. Flour your hands (and your work surface, if needed). Use the palms of your hands to gently press and roll the loaf into a long cylinder. Start with your hands in the middle of the loaf and gradually move them to the outer edge of the baguette as you roll, extending it to the full size of a typical baguette, about 14 inches. Repeat with the remaining dough to make four baguettes.

6. Transfer the shaped baguettes to a the prepared baking sheet and let rise for 20 to 25 minutes. Bake until golden brown, 25 to 30 minutes.

Sonoma Chicken Salad on Whole-Wheat Baguettes

Mix chopped cooked chicken with mayonnaise, sliced seedless grapes, and minced shallot. Season with salt and freshly ground black pepper. Serve on whole-wheat baguettes (page 63).

RECOMMENDED DOUGH: *Honey Whole-Wheat*

Black Forest Ham and Brie on Baguette

Spread a thick layer of mayonnaise and Dijon mustard on a split baguette (page 63). Layer with slices of creamy Brie and Black Forest ham. Slice and serve.

RECOMMENDED DOUGH: *Basic*

Lemon-Butterbean Puree with Arugula on Baguette

In a food processor or blender, puree 2 cups cooked, cooled butter beans (about 1 16-ounce can, rinsed), ¼ cup extra-virgin olive oil, 2 cloves garlic, 1 small handful fresh basil leaves, and the juice of 1 lemon until smooth and very creamy. Season with salt and freshly ground black pepper. Spread a thick layer of the butter bean mixture on a Quick Baguette (page 63) split in half lengthwise and toasted. Top with a drizzle of extra-virgin olive oil, a large handful of fresh arugula, some shaved Parmesan, lemon zest, and more salt and pepper. Slice and serve.

RECOMMENDED DOUGHS: *Basic, Sourdough*

Deconstructed Panzanella with Burrata

Cut two 4-ounce rounds of fresh burrata mozzarella cheese into quarters and arrange in the center of a platter. Surround with 3 cups halved cherry or grape tomatoes, and 1 large handful torn fresh basil. Cube 1 Quick Baguette (page 63) and drizzle the whole thing with 3 tablespoons extra-virgin olive oil and 2 tablespoons balsamic vinegar. Season with salt and freshly ground black pepper. Let the flavors meld for 15 to 20 minutes, then serve.

RECOMMENDED DOUGHS: *Basic, Sourdough*

Ricotta–Red Pepper Crostini with Basil

Slice a Quick Baguette (page 63) into ½-inch pieces. Brush each piece liberally with extra-virgin olive oil and arrange on a baking sheet. Toast in an oven preheated to 375° F until crisp, 8 to 10 minutes. Let cool for a few minutes, then spread each toast with ricotta (preferably whole-milk), and top each one with a few thin slices of roasted red bell pepper, and some chopped fresh basil. Season with salt and freshly ground black pepper. Serve immediately.

RECOMMENDED DOUGHS: *Basic, Sourdough*

Garlic Croutons

In a blender or food processor, puree ¼ cup extra-virgin olive oil and 3 garlic cloves until smooth (the liquid will look creamy and almost white). Place 2 cups cubed Quick Baguette (page 63; preferably a few days old) in a large bowl. Pour the garlic-oil mixture over the bread and use your hands to mix well, making sure each bread cube is coated. Spread coated cubes on an ungreased baking sheet. Sprinkle lightly with salt. Bake in an oven heated to 450°F for 12 to 15 minutes. Check and flip croutons over halfway through, so they are evenly browned. Serve warm or cooled.

RECOMMENDED DOUGHS: *Basic, Sourdough*

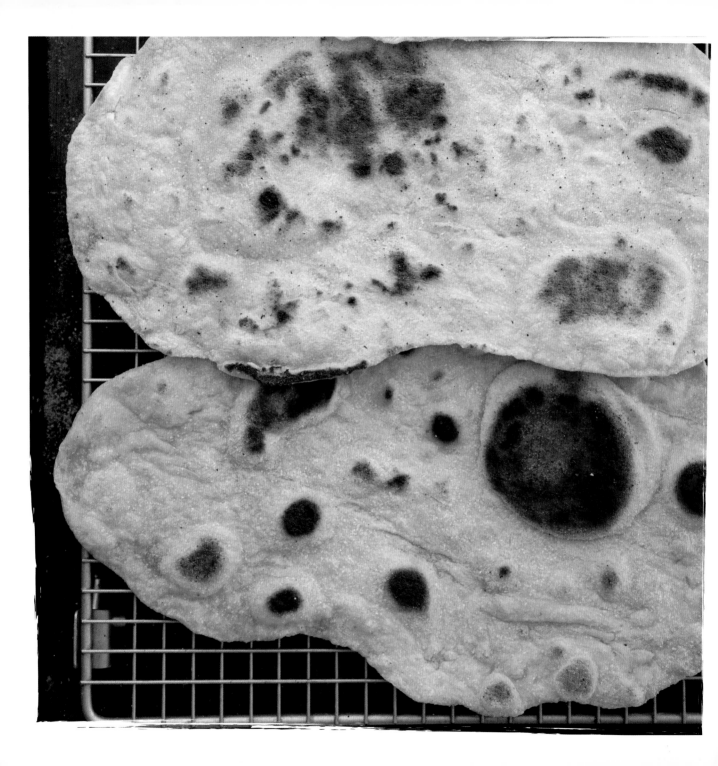

PREP TIME: 25 minutes
TOTAL TIME: 1 hour, 10 minutes
YIELD: 12 naans (serves 6 to 12)

Basic Naan Use this as a base for an Indian-inspired sandwich or cut it into wedges and serve with sliced vegetables for a quick, unique appetizer.

Flour for rolling

1 recipe pizza dough

2 tablespoons butter, melted

RECOMMENDED DOUGHS: *Basic, Pumpkin, Honey Whole-Wheat*

1. Turn the dough out onto a floured work surface. Using a bench scraper or a knife, cut the dough into 12 even pieces. Roll each piece into a ball and place all of them on a well-floured surface (leaving a few inches of space between each one), and cover with a floured cloth. Alternatively, place each ball of dough in an individual, covered pint-sized deli container. Allow dough to rise at room temperature until doubled in volume, about 2 hours.

2. Heat a large, dry frying pan over medium-high heat. Working with two to three balls of dough at a time, stretch each piece of dough into an oblong roughly 10-by-6 inches. (You can do this using your hands or a rolling pin.) Once you have two or three pieces stretched, lay them out on the pan and cook without moving them until the bottom is charred in spots and light golden brown. Flip with a large spatula, or with tongs, and cook until the second side is charred and browned.

3. Remove the naan from the grill and immediately brush with melted butter. Transfer the naan to a large plate and cover it with a clean dish towel while you cook the remaining bread.

Naan with Yogurt Dip

Combine 1 cup plain Greek-style yogurt (any fat percentage), 2 teaspoons curry powder, and 1 tablespoon honey in a small bowl. Stir well and then season with salt and freshly ground black pepper. Serve with either Basic Naan (page 67), cut into wedges, or Pumpkin Naan Chips (recipe follows).

RECOMMENDED DOUGHS: *Basic, Pumpkin, Honey Whole-Wheat*

Pumpkin Naan Chips

Prepare the Basic Nan recipe (page 67) using pumpkin dough. Cut 4 rounds of the pumpkin naan into wedges (I like to try to get 8 to 10 wedges out of each round.) Spread evenly on a baking sheet and brush with olive oil, melted butter or melted clarified butter (ghee). Bake in an oven heated to 450°F for 6 to 7 minutes on each side or until golden brown and crisp. Sprinkle lightly with salt and smoked paprika.

RECOMMENDED DOUGH: *Pumpkin*

East Indian Wraps

Curry-rubbed-and-grilled chicken, fish, paneer (an Indian cheese), or tofu along with cooked basmati rice make great fillings for these delicious wraps. Prepare the Basic Nan recipe (page 67) using the dough of your choice. Layer on plain yogurt; thinly sliced vegetables such as carrots, cucumbers, radishes, steamed beets, and red onions; then top with fresh, chopped cilantro. Fold the naan in half and serve.

RECOMMENDED DOUGH: *Basic, Pumpkin, Honey Whole-Wheat*

Tandoori-Style Chicken on Pumpkin Naan

Prepare the Basic Naan recipe (page 67) using pumpkin dough. Stir chopped grilled chicken together with a dash of soy sauce, 1/2 teaspoon curry powder, a drizzle of honey, and freshly ground black pepper to taste. Serve folded into pumpkin naan with chopped lettuce and fresh cilantro.

RECOMMENDED DOUGH: *Pumpkin*

PREP TIME: 35 minutes
TOTAL TIME: 55 minutes
YIELD: 20 folded buns (serves 5 to 10)

Chinese Folded Steamed Buns

David Chang, chef behind the famed Momofuku culinary empire, has brought the classic Chinese folded bun to the forefront of the contemporary American food scene. After trying the recipe in his best-selling cookbook, *Momofuku* (Clarkson Potter, 2009), I discovered that the dough for folded steamed buns (flour, yeast, salt, and a little fat) is nearly identical to that of basic pizza dough.

Using my own recipe for dough, I adapted his method for rolling, folding, and steaming the buns.

These are terrific with pulled pork or chicken, seared ahi tuna, or grilled tofu.

Flour for rolling

1 recipe pizza dough

Canola or vegetable oil

RECOMMENDED DOUGH: *Basic*

1. Cut a large sheet of parchment paper into twenty 4-inch pieces, and set aside.

2. On a floured surface, divide the dough into 20 small pieces. Gently roll each piece into a round ball. Use a floured rolling pin to gently roll a dough ball out into a 4-inch oval.

3. Lightly grease a chopstick or the handle of a wooden spoon with the canola or vegetable oil.

4. Hold the dough oval in your hand, and place the greased chopstick or wooden spoon in the center of the oval. Fold the oval in half, and gently withdraw the chopstick or spoon handle.

5. Place the folded dough on a parchment square and set aside.

continued

6. Repeat with the remaining dough and parchment squares, until you have 20 parchment-lined folded doughs.

7. Arrange the folded doughs on their papers in 2 lines of 10 and drape loosely with plastic wrap. Let rise for 20 minutes.

8. Prepare your steamer on the stove. Working in batches, so as not to overcrowd the doughs, steam on the parchment for 12 minutes.

9. The buns can be eaten plain or filled and served immediately, or brought to room temperature and transferred to an airtight container and frozen for up to 3 months.

Quick Chinese Pork Buns

Prepare the Steamed Buns as directed on page 71. Stir together 1 clove minced garlic, $\frac{1}{2}$ teaspoon minced ginger, $\frac{1}{8}$ cup hoisin sauce, and 1 teaspoon Asian chili sauce (like sambal oelek or Sriracha) until well combined. Pour over 2 cups hot, cooked, shredded pork and stir well. Fill each folded bun with 1 to 2 tablespoons of the pork mixture, and top with thinly sliced cucumber, shredded carrots, a sprig of fresh cilantro, and more hot sauce to taste.

RECOMMENDED DOUGH: *Basic*

Puffy Fry Bread

These breads are wonderful as they are, but I like to use them as a base for Indian wraps! Simply heap each fry bread with cooked crumbled meat (or tofu), cheese, lettuce, sour cream, guacamole, and hot sauce.

You can also sprinkle them with powdered sugar for a sweet version.

1 recipe pizza dough

Flour for rolling

Vegetable oil for frying

RECOMMENDED DOUGH: *Basic*

1. Divide the dough into 6 balls and roll each one out into a 5-inch round on a lightly floured surface.

2. Meanwhile, heat about ½ inch oil in a large skillet to about 375°F, or almost smoking hot.

3. Carefully slip a round of dough into the hot oil. Gently press it down with a fork or a chopstick so it is submerged in the oil. The bread will bubble up impressively as it cooks. When the first side is browned, turn and brown the second side. Using tongs or chopsticks, remove the cooked bread from the oil and place it on paper towels or a clean brown paper bag to drain.

4. Continue frying until all the fry breads are cooked. Serve warm.

PREP TIME: 20 minutes
TOTAL TIME: 45 minutes
YIELD: 10 dinner rolls (serves 10)

Rosemary-Garlic Dinner Rolls

I dream about these crusty, buttery rolls. They're so tasty that I like to make sure they get all the attention they deserve, so I serve them with a fare that won't outshine them, like a simple soup and a green salad.

4 tablespoons butter, melted

2 cloves garlic, minced

2 tablespoons fresh rosemary, chopped

½ teaspoon salt

1 pound fresh pizza dough

RECOMMENDED DOUGHS: *Basic, Herb-Garlic, Honey Whole-Wheat, Egg*

1. Combine the butter, garlic, rosemary, and salt. Brush about half of the mixture onto an 8-inch pie plate or springform pan.

2. Divide the dough into 10 equal pieces. Shape into balls. Place 2 balls in the center of the pie plate or springform pan and the remaining 8 around the outside. Brush each ball lightly with the melted butter mixture as you go so they don't stick to one another. Brush the tops of the arranged dough balls with the remaining butter mixture.

3. Cover with lightly oiled plastic wrap and let rise for 25 minutes.

4. Preheat the oven to 375°F. Remove plastic. Bake until golden, 25 to 30 minutes, and serve warm.

PREP TIME: 35 minutes
TOTAL TIME: 1 hour
YIELD: 12 pita rounds (serves 10)

Fresh Pita Bread

Kick your falafel up several notches with oven-fresh pita! Hot, puffy, and just chewy enough, these are perfect for holding traditional Middle Eastern ingredients or for cutting into wedges and serving with hummus. Once you learn how easy and significantly more delicious it is to make your own pita, you'll never go back to the store-bought variety again.

This recipe is adapted from one on Deb Perelman's phenomenal blog, *Smitten Kitchen*.

1 recipe pizza dough

Flour for rolling

RECOMMENDED DOUGHS: *Basic, Honey Whole-Wheat*

1. Preheat the oven to 475°F one hour before baking. Have an oven shelf at the lowest level and place a baking stone, cast-iron skillet, or baking sheet on it before preheating.

2. To shape the dough, begin by cutting it into 12 pieces. Work with one piece at a time, keeping the rest covered with a damp cloth. On a lightly floured surface, with lightly floured hands, shape each piece into a ball and then flatten it into a disk. Cover the dough with lightly oiled plastic and allow it to rest for 20 minutes at room temperature.

3. Then, using your hands or a rolling pin, shape each disk into a thin round (about ½ inch thick).

4. Allow the dough rounds to rest, uncovered, for 10 minutes.

5. Quickly place a few of the dough rounds directly on the stone, in the skillet, or on the baking sheet, and bake for 3 minutes. The pitas should be completely puffed but not beginning to brown. The dough will not puff well if it is not moist enough. If you need to moisten it, spray it once or twice with water in a spray bottle.

6. Proceed with the remaining dough, baking 3 or 4 pieces at a time. Then, using a large spatula, transfer the pita breads to a clean towel to stay soft and warm. Allow the oven to reheat for 5 minutes between batches. The pitas can be reheated for about 30 seconds in a hot oven before serving.

7. Alternatively, to cook the pitas on the stove top, preheat a griddle or cast-iron skillet over medium-high heat. Lightly grease the surface and cook the pitas one at a time. Cook for about 20 seconds, turn the dough, and continue cooking for 1 minute, or until big bubbles appear. Turn the dough again and cook until the dough balloons. If the dough begins to brown, lower the heat.

PREP TIME: 10 minutes
COOK TIME: 24 minutes
YIELD: 1 6x8-inch loaf (serves 6 to 8)

Rosemary–Sun-Dried Tomato Focaccia This

quick-but-very-special bread recipe is your express route to an out-of-control-good sandwich. Split a square in half and layer it with meats (I recommend prosciutto or salami), veggies, cheeses, and a nice drizzle of quality extra-virgin olive oil, and you'll be the envy of your workplace or school cafeteria lunch crowd.

Or, simply slice the warm focaccia into dinner roll–sized squares and serve in a bread basket with dinner.

Flour for baking sheet and rolling

1 recipe pizza dough

2 tablespoons extra-virgin olive oil

1 teaspoon each salt and freshly ground black pepper

2 tablespoons chopped sun-dried tomatoes

1 tablespoon fresh rosemary leaves

⅓ cup shredded (not grated) Parmesan

RECOMMENDED DOUGHS: *Basic, Herb-Garlic, Sourdough*

1. Preheat the oven to 400°F. Lightly flour (or line with parchment paper) a baking sheet.

2. On another lightly floured surface, shape the pizza dough into an approximately 6-by-8 inch rectangle. Transfer the dough rectangle to the prepared baking sheet.

3. Use your fingertips to make light indentations all over the top of the dough (it should look like a bumpy landscape). Drizzle with the olive oil and use your hands to rub the sides of the dough with oil as well.

4. Season the top of the dough with salt and pepper and then gently press the sun-dried tomatoes into the dough. Next, sprinkle the bread with the rosemary and Parmesan and bake until the cheese is golden brown and the focaccia sounds hollow when tapped gently on the bottom, 22 to 24 minutes. Let cool slightly and then cut into squares and serve.

Muffaletta on Focaccia

Prepare the focaccia as directed on page 78. Use a rubber spatula to spread olive salad or tapenade on the inside of each half of the bread. Layer the bottom slice of bread with salami and then top with the slices of mozzarella or provolone. Top the cheese with sliced bell pepper. Cover the whole thing with the second half of the bread and press down firmly. Wrap the sandwich tightly with plastic wrap or aluminum foil and leave at room temperature for 30 to 60 minutes before serving.

RECOMMENDED DOUGHS: *Basic, Sourdough*

Chicken-Pesto Panini on Focaccia

Prepare the focaccia as directed on page 78. Preheat a panini grill or 2 heavy frying pans. Slice a whole foccacia into quarters. Slice each quarter of focaccia bread in half horizontally (as if you were splitting a roll). Spread each half with pesto. Layer bottom halves with equal amounts of cubed chicken, cubed bell pepper, and shredded mozzarella cheese. Top with remaining focaccia halves, forming 4 sandwiches, and grill for 5 minutes on the grill or between the two preheated frying pans. If using frying pans, weight the top with a few filled cans while the panini grills. Serve hot.

RECOMMENDED DOUGH: *Basic*

The Ultimate Thanksgiving Leftover Sandwich

Prepare the focaccia as directed on page 78. Heat 1 tablespoon extra-virgin olive oil in a grill pan or frying pan over high heat. Add the slices from 1 orange and 1 onion, and cook for 2 to 3 minutes on each side, or until medium color develops and the oranges and onions become quite fragrant. Remove the pan from heat. Spread left over cranberry sauce and creamy goat cheese on one side of a horizontally cut and toasted piece of focaccia bread. Layer leftover turkey, fresh or cooked greens, orange slices, and onions on the goat cheese covered slices. Top each with a slice of the cranberry and goat cheese–covered bread and secure with a toothpick. Repeat process with remaining ingredients.

RECOMMENDED DOUGH: *Basic*

PREP TIME: 1 hour, 15 minutes
TOTAL TIME: 2 hours
YIELD: One 12-inch loaf (serves 4 to 6)

Challah

Rich egg pizza dough lends itself nicely to fresh challah. I like to braid it as I would hair, but there are lots of ways to get fancy with your challah. Check out Tori Avey's phenomenal website, The Shiksa in the Kitchen (www.theshiksa.com), for a great primer on challah braiding.

Flour for baking sheet and rolling

1 recipe pizza dough

1 egg

2 tablespoons water

Sesame seeds or poppy seeds (optional)

RECOMMENDED DOUGH: *Egg*

1. Preheat the oven to 375°F. Lightly flour a baking sheet.

2. On another floured surface, divide the dough into 3 equal pieces. Roll each piece into a 12-inch snake shape.

3. Braid the pieces together and place the braid on the prepared baking sheet. Let rise for 20 minutes.

4. In a small bowl, beat the egg with the water. Use a pastry brush to brush the braid with the egg wash. Sprinkle with the seeds, if using, and bake until the bread is golden brown and sounds hollow when tapped on the bottom, 35 to 40 minutes.

Maine Lobster Rolls on Challah

Prepare the challah as directed above. Roughly chop about ⅓ pound freshly steamed and cooled lobster tail meat and transfer to a bowl. Stir in 1½ tablespoons mayonnaise, a squeeze of lemon, 2 chopped scallions, a dash of paprika and salt and freshly ground black pepper to taste. Lightly butter the tops and bottoms of 4 thick slices of challah, and then toast on both sides on a hot frying pan or griddle over medium heat until golden brown. To serve, place a slice of Boston or butter lettuce on a slice of toasted challah, top with half of the lobster mixture, and then top with a second slice of toasted challah. Repeat to make the second sandwich. Serve immediately.

RECOMMENDED DOUGH: *Egg*

CHAPTER 4

PIZZAS, CALZONES, AND PIADINAS

And then, of course, there's pizza.

Thin-crust pizza, along with its folded cousin the calzone, and its Chicago cousin, deep dish, are ultimately what we think of when pizza dough comes to mind. They conjure memories of college all-nighters, visits to a favorite pizzeria, or the streets of New York (or Chicago!); pizza holds meaning for just about everyone.

One of my favorite ways to serve pizza and calzones is by having a pizza party. I make a big batch of dough (sometimes several kinds) and set out sauces, cheeses, and toppings. I let guests make personal pizzas and calzones (line pans with parchment paper and use a marker to write the pizza-maker's name next to his or her creation before baking).

Sometimes I add a salad or two, but more often than not, the pizza and calzones are plenty.

Whether it's a pizza party for a group or a calzone soiree for two, these recipes will guide you. You'll find basic recipes for thin-crust pizza, deep-dish pizza, and calzones, plus several flavor combinations and specialty pies. As always, I encourage you to experiment with your own ideas!

PREP TIME: 15 minutes
TOTAL TIME: 30 minutes
YIELD: One 12-inch pizza
(serves 3 to 4)

Basic Thin-Crust Pizza

When most people think of pizza, this is usually what comes to mind: crisp-yet-chewy crust with a thin layer of sauce, a variety of toppings, and bubbly, melted cheese. It's what we grew up on. It's what we order to be delivered for lunch, dinner, and late-night snacking.

And, as it turns out, it's easy to make. All you need is dough, sauce, cheese (or not), toppings, salt, and pepper. Chances are, you already have everything you need to make homemade pizza, so say good-bye to the frozen stuff!

This is your basic pizza template. Use it to make the suggested pizza flavor combinations I've included on pages 89 and 90, or as a canvas for your own creativity.

Flour for baking sheet and rolling

1 recipe pizza dough

½ to ⅔ cup sauce of choice (see page 12)

1 cup shredded or sliced mozzarella cheese

1½ cups toppings of choice

Salt and freshly ground black pepper

RECOMMENDED DOUGHS: *Basic, Honey Whole-Wheat, Gluten-Free*

1. Preheat the oven to 475°F. Lightly flour a baking sheet or pizza pan and set aside.

2. On another lightly floured surface, roll the pizza dough into a 14-inch round. Spread the dough with the sauce, sprinkle the cheese, then scatter the toppings over the top. (Remember not to go too heavy.) Finally, add a light sprinkling of salt and pepper.

3. Bake until dough is golden brown and the cheese and toppings are bubbly, 13 to 15 minutes. Let cool slightly and then slice and serve.

Classic Marinara

Spread a thin layer of tomato sauce over a 14-inch round of dough. Top with medallions of fresh mozzarella di bufala, thin slices of fresh basil, and a drizzle of quality extra-virgin olive oil. Bake according to recipe directions on page 86.

RECOMMENDED DOUGHS: *Basic, Honey Whole-Wheat, Sourdough, Gluten-Free*

Margherita

Top a 14-inch round of dough with two medium roasted tomatoes. Top with medallions of fresh mozzarella di bufala, thin slices of fresh basil, and a drizzle of quality extra-virgin olive oil. Bake according to recipe directions on page 86.

RECOMMENDED DOUGHS: *Basic, Herb-Garlic, Sourdough, Gluten-Free*

Club Med

Spread prepared tapenade over a 14-inch round of dough and top with crumbled feta and strips of chopped red pepper. Bake according to recipe directions on page 86. Add fresh chopped flat-leaf parsley and red pepper flakes after baking, if desired.

RECOMMENDED DOUGHS: *Basic, Honey Whole-Wheat, Sourdough, Gluten-Free*

The Frisky Goat

Spread pesto over a 14-inch round of dough. Scatter creamy dollops of fresh goat cheese evenly over the pesto and then top with a light sprinkling of chopped scallions or chives. Bake according to recipe directions on page 86.

RECOMMENDED DOUGHS: *Basic, Honey Whole-Wheat, Sourdough, Gluten-Free*

Figgy Gorgonzola

Simply smear prepared fig jam over a 14-inch round of dough. Top with crumbled Gorgonzola and strew soft, sweet caramelized onions over the top. Bake according to recipe directions on page 86.

RECOMMENDED DOUGHS: *Basic, Sourdough, Gluten-Free*

The Elephant Walk

Simply spread prepared peanut sauce over a 14-inch round of dough and bake according to recipe directions on page 86. Top with cooked, shredded chicken, shredded carrots, sliced scallions, chopped cilantro, and a drizzle of Asian chili sauce (like Sriracha), if desired.

RECOMMENDED DOUGHS: *Basic, Pumpkin, Honey Whole-Wheat, Sourdough, Gluten-Free*

Jalapeño Popper

Smear ¾ cup (6 ounces) of cream cheese onto a 14-inch round of dough. Top with 1 cup shredded sharp cheddar cheese, 2 roasted and sliced jalapeños (or canned green chilies if you prefer less heat), 3 slices cooked, crumbled bacon, and 3 green onions, chopped. Bake according to recipe directions on page 86.

RECOMMENDED DOUGHS: *Basic, Sourdough, Gluten-Free*

PREP TIME: 20 minutes

TOTAL TIME: 35 minutes

YIELD: One 12-inch pizza
(serves 3 to 4)

Pepperoni Pizza with Roasted Tomato Sauce

The roasted tomatoes bring a welcome sweetness that complements the spicy pepperoni nicely. Feel free to add another topping or two; sliced button mushrooms and green peppers work well here.

Flour for baking sheet and rolling

½ recipe pizza dough

1 cup Roasted Tomato Sauce (page 12)

1½ cups shredded mozzarella cheese

About 12 slices pepperoni

¼ cup fresh basil

Salt and freshly ground black pepper

RECOMMENDED DOUGHS: *Basic, Honey Whole-Wheat, Sourdough, Gluten-Free*

1. Preheat the oven to 450°F. Lightly flour a baking sheet and set aside.

2. On another lightly floured surface, roll the pizza dough into the desired shape (I made mine oblong) and transfer to the prepared baking sheet. Top with the tomato sauce, cheese, pepperoni, basil, and salt and pepper.

3. Bake until the crust is golden brown and the cheese is very bubbly, 13 to 15 minutes. Cut into wedges and serve.

PREP TIME: 20 minutes
TOTAL TIME: 30 minutes
YIELD: one 12-inch pizza
(serves 3 to 4)

Vegetable Pizza with Roasted Tomato Sauce

This deeply flavorful pizza pleases vegetarians and meat eaters alike. It's a meal in itself, but you could add a fresh soup or a crisp green salad to put it over the top.

Flour for baking sheet and rolling

½ recipe pizza dough

1 cup Roasted Tomato Sauce (page 12)

1½ cups shredded mozzarella cheese

¼ cup sliced black olives

½ cup thinly sliced broccoli

⅓ cup thinly sliced mushrooms

Extra-virgin olive oil for drizzling

Salt and freshly ground black pepper

pepper

¼ cup fresh basil

RECOMMENDED DOUGHS: *Basic, Honey Whole-Wheat, Sourdough, Gluten-Free*

1. Preheat the oven to 475°F. Lightly flour a baking sheet or pizza pan and set aside.

2. On another floured surface, roll out the pizza into a 12-inch round. Transfer to the prepared pan and set aside.

3. Spoon tomato sauce over the pizza dough, leaving a ½-inch border for the crust. Scatter the cheese over the sauce, spacing evenly then add, olives, broccoli, and mushrooms.

4. Bake until the crust is golden brown and the cheese is bubbly, 12 to 15 minutes. Top with a light drizzle of olive oil, salt, pepper, and a shower of fresh basil. Cut into wedges and serve.

PREP TIME: 30 minutes
TOTAL TIME: 50 minutes
YIELD: One 12-inch pizza
(serves 3 to 4)

Breakfast Pizza

This is a complete breakfast in pizza form. You've got eggs, bacon, cheese, and toast. I like it with fruit, coffee, and the Sunday paper, but you could brunch it up a bit by serving it with a green salad. Feel free to cook the eggs longer if you don't like them runny.

Flour for baking sheet and rolling

½ recipe pizza dough

6 strips bacon

1 medium onion, sliced

2 cups grated mozzarella cheese

4 large eggs

Salt and freshly ground black pepper

2 scallions, thinly sliced

RECOMMENDED DOUGHS: *Basic, Pumpkin, Honey Whole-Wheat, Egg, Gluten-Free*

1. Preheat the oven to 475°F. Lightly flour a baking sheet and set aside.

2. Fry the bacon in a large frying pan over medium-high heat until crisp. Cool on a paper towel–lined plate; chop roughly and retain the bacon grease.

3. Meanwhile, cook the onions in the leftover grease over medium heat, just until they brown. Drain and set aside.

4. On a lightly floured surface, roll the dough out into a 12-inch round. Transfer the round to the prepared baking sheet.

5. Sprinkle the dough with the mozzarella, bacon, and onions. Crack the eggs over the top and season with salt and pepper.

6. Bake for 7 to 8 minutes and then rotate halfway and bake for another 5 minutes. (This helps make sure the eggs cook evenly.)

7. Sprinkle with the chopped scallions, cut into wedges, and serve, making sure everyone gets some of the egg.

Crispy Scallion Pizza

This straightforward-yet-unique pizza showcases my latest culinary obsession: fried scallions. I slice the scallions (I use the whole thing—both white and green parts), fry them until brown and crispy in a little extra-virgin olive oil, and then lightly salt them (don't forget the salt—it brings out the scallions' delicate flavor). The sweet-yet-bright tomato-parsley sauce is the perfect base for these little lovelies, and the resulting pie is full of flavor yet understated.

Flour for baking sheet and rolling

Extra-virgin olive oil

8 scallions, cut lengthwise and then into 1-inch strips

Salt and freshly ground black pepper

1 large handful fresh flat-leaf parsley leaves

2 tablespoons tomato paste

3 cloves garlic

½ recipe pizza dough

4 ounces fontina or mozzarella, thinly sliced

Red chili flakes (optional, but highly recommended)

RECOMMENDED DOUGHS: *Basic, Honey Whole-Wheat, Sourdough, Gluten-Free*

1. Preheat the oven to 475°F. Lightly flour a baking sheet or pizza pan and set aside.

2. Heat 4 tablespoons olive oil in a medium frying pan over medium-high heat. Add the scallions and cook, turning occasionally, for 1 to 2 minutes, or until they lose most of their greenness and become golden brown and crispy. Drain on paper towels and sprinkle lightly with salt.

3. In a blender or food processor, combine 2 tablespoons olive oil with the parsley, tomato paste, and garlic and puree to form a slightly chunky paste. Season with salt and pepper and set aside.

4. On another lightly floured surface, use your hands to stretch and shape the pizza dough into an 8-inch round or square (or whatever shape you'd like) and transfer to the prepared baking pan. Spread the sauce over the pizza, leaving a ½-inch border for the crust. Then spread the cheese slices evenly over the pizza.

5. Bake until crust is golden brown and lightly charred, 10 to 12 minutes. Top with red chili flakes and the fried scallions, cut into wedges, and serve.

PREP TIME: 25 minutes
TOTAL TIME: 40 minutes
YIELD: One 12-inch pizza
(serves 3 to 4)

White Pizza with Brussels Sprouts I know; I know.

You claim not to like Brussels sprouts. You say they taste bitter and have a mushy texture. Well, you know what? You're wrong. Dead wrong. You just haven't had them prepared correctly.

You've eaten them overboiled without substantial seasoning. Well-prepared pan-roasted Brussels sprouts are sublime—sweetly caramelized on the outside, with a layered, almost-spicy flavor. Try them on this easy-to-love white pizza. You'll see.

Flour for baking sheet and rolling

2 tablespoons extra-virgin olive oil

About 8 Brussels sprouts, quartered lengthwise

3 cloves garlic, chopped

Salt and freshly ground black pepper

½ recipe pizza dough

3 tablespoons half-and-half

¾ cup shredded white cheddar cheese

Crushed red chili flakes

RECOMMENDED DOUGHS: *Basic, Honey Whole-Wheat, Sourdough, Egg, Gluten-Free*

1. Preheat the oven to 475°F. Lightly flour a baking sheet or pizza pan.

2. Heat 1 tablespoon olive oil in a medium frying pan over medium-high heat. Add the Brussels sprouts and cook for 3 to 4 minutes, stirring occasionally, until they begin to brown. Add the garlic and cook for another minute. Season with salt and pepper and remove from heat.

3. On another lightly floured surface, roll the dough into a 12-inch round. Transfer to the prepared baking sheet. Use a pastry brush to spread about 2 tablespoons olive oil over the dough. Use the same brush to spread the half-and-half over the oiled dough. Top with the cheese and spread the Brussels sprouts–garlic mixture over the cheese. Sprinkle with the chili flakes.

4. Bake until the cheese is bubbly and the crust is golden brown, 12 to 15 minutes. Cut the pizza into wedges and serve.

Note: *The half-and-half will thicken in the oven, yielding a creamy white base for your pizza—don't worry if it looks soupy when you put it in to bake.*

Egg and Asparagus Pizza

So, basically, I went to the farmers' market and then turned my purchases into a pizza. The herbs, garlic, cheese, vegetables, and eggs are all locally sourced and fresh. If you'd like to avoid the dairy, the cheese can be omitted and still yield tasty results.

Flour for baking sheet and rolling

1 handful cilantro

1 handful flat-leaf parsley

3 tablespoons extra-virgin olive oil

2 cloves garlic, peeled

2 tablespoons raw almonds

Salt and freshly ground black pepper

6 stalks asparagus

½ recipe pizza dough

½ cup grated white cheddar or mozzarella cheese

2 to 3 eggs

1 tomato, diced

Crushed red chili flakes (optional)

RECOMMENDED DOUGHS: *Basic, Pumpkin, Honey Whole-Wheat, Sourdough, Gluten-Free*

1. Preheat the oven to 475°F. Lightly flour a baking sheet or pizza pan and set aside.

2. Place herbs, olive oil, garlic, and almonds in a food processor or blender and puree into a slightly chunky pesto. Season with salt and pepper.

3. On a cutting board, shave the asparagus. Lay a stalk on the board and carefully run a vegetable peeler over the length of the stalk, creating a thin strip. Continue until all that is left is a thin strip of asparagus and repeat with the remaining asparagus. Set aside with other pizza ingredients.

4. On a lightly floured surface, use a rolling pin to roll the dough out into a 12-inch round. Transfer to the prepared baking sheet.

5. Spread the pesto over the base of the dough, leaving a 1-inch border for the crust. Sprinkle with the cheese and crack the eggs over it. Top with shaved asparagus and diced tomato. Bake until the crust is crisp and browned on the edges, 10 to 12 minutes.

6. Sprinkle with crushed red chili flakes, if desired. Cut into wedges and serve, making sure everyone gets some of the egg.

Pesto–Goat Cheese Pizza

For this simple pizza, I call for goat cheese and prepared pesto, although you may opt to prepare your own pesto (see page 11). The slightly tart flavor of the goat cheese blends deliciously with the peppery-sweet basil

Flour for baking sheet and rolling

1 recipe pizza dough

¼ cup prepared or homemade basil pesto

1 cup fresh goat cheese, crumbled

½ teaspoon salt

RECOMMENDED DOUGHS: *Basic, Honey Whole-Wheat, Sourdough, Gluten-Free*

1. Preheat the oven to 475°F. Lightly flour a baking sheet or pizza pan and set aside.

2. Dust another clean, flat surface with flour. Using a floured rolling pin (or a wine bottle, in a pinch), roll the dough out into a 12-inch round and transfer it onto the prepared baking sheet. Spread the pesto evenly over the dough, leaving a 1-inch border for the crust. Sprinkle the goat cheese evenly over the top of the pesto. Season lightly with salt.

3. Bake until the crust is golden brown and the top of the pizza is browned in spots, 12 to 15 minutes. Cut into wedges and serve.

PREP TIME: 30 minutes
TOTAL TIME: 45 minutes
YIELD: One 12-inch pizza
(serves 2 to 4)

Egg and Seared-Spinach Pizza

One warm spring day, Delfina Pizzeria in San Francisco, one of my favorite places to find both pizza and inspiration, featured a garlicky broccoli rabe pie topped with a whole egg. It was the first time I had encountered egg on a pizza. When we were served, I was delighted by how the yolk oozed out and combined with the other ingredients to form an impromptu sauce atop the pizza. This is my take on it.

Flour for baking sheet and rolling

1 cup cherry tomatoes, halved

3 cloves garlic, chopped

2 tablespoons extra-virgin olive oil

1 small bunch flat-leaf Italian parsley, chopped, a bit reserved for garnish

Salt and freshly ground black pepper

½ recipe pizza dough

¾ cup shredded Asiago cheese

2 cups spinach, rinsed and dried

2 tablespoons toasted, sliced almonds (see note page 29)

1 egg

RECOMMENDED DOUGHS: *Basic, Pumpkin, Honey Whole-Wheat, Egg, Gluten-Free*

1. Preheat the oven to 475°F. Lightly flour a baking sheet or pizza pan and set aside.

2. In a small bowl, combine the tomatoes, garlic, olive oil, and parsley. Season well with salt and pepper. Set aside.

3. On another floured surface, roll the pizza dough out into a 9-inch round. Transfer to the prepared baking sheet. Spread the tomato mixture over the dough, leaving a ½ inch border for the crust. Top with the Asiago cheese, spinach, and almonds. Gently crack an egg in the middle of the pizza, being careful to keep the yolk intact.

4. Bake until the edges of the crust are brown and the cheese is melted and bubbly, 12 to 15 minutes. Just before serving, run a knife gently through the top of the still-runny yolk and let it run over the pizza. Garnish with more parsley. Cut into wedges and serve.

PREP TIME: 25 minutes
TOTAL TIME: 35 minutes
YIELD: Four 6-inch pizzas (serves 4)

Grilled Eggplant Flatbread Pizza

If you claim to hate eggplant, I double-dog dare you to try this pizza. Hell, I triple-dog dare you. Seriously. That slimy, spongy texture that so many people associate with this innocent vegetable disappears when the eggplant is roasted over an open flame. It's replaced with a silky, smoky, rich result, substantial enough to act in place of tomato sauce on these grilled flatbread pizzas.

This dish would work well with feta or goat cheese in place of the mozzarella and with parsley or basil in place of the mint. Feel free to experiment.

Also, there's something about grilled flatbread that just begs for al fresco dining . . . maybe with a glass of chilled Prosecco.

1 medium eggplant, 7 to 8 inches long

2 cloves garlic, finely minced

1 tablespoon extra-virgin olive oil plus more for grill

Salt and freshly ground black pepper

Flour for rolling

½ recipe pizza dough

4 ounces fresh mozzarella (mozzarella di bufala), sliced into thin medallion-size pieces

RECOMMENDED DOUGHS: *Basic, Honey Whole-Wheat, Sourdough, Egg*

1. Bring the flame of a burner on a gas stove or an outside grill up to high. Hold the eggplant with tongs. (Make sure the tongs are heatproof where your hands go; otherwise put a towel or potholder between your hands and the tongs.) Hold the eggplant over the flame for 2 to 3 minutes per side, rotating to make sure the entire eggplant gets roasted. The skin should be completely brown and blistered, and the flesh should be very soft. Once the eggplant is completely roasted, run it under cold water until cool enough to touch and then carefully peel off the skin and discard. Place the soft, skinless flesh in a small bowl and mash with the back of a fork until very soft. Stir in the garlic, and 1 tablespoon of the olive oil. Season with salt and pepper. Set aside.

2 Roma tomatoes, sliced

Few pinches red chili flakes

1 small bunch mint leaves, chopped

2. On a lightly floured surface, divide the pizza dough into 4 small balls. Use a rolling pin to roll each one into a 6-inch round and set aside.

3. Brush a grill or grill pan lightly with olive oil and bring to medium-high heat. Carefully lay dough rounds on the surface of the grill (working in batches if using a grill pan or a small grill). Allow the dough to cook on one side until dark grill marks appear and the crust becomes somewhat crisp. Flip using tongs and spread a thick layer of the eggplant mixture over each dough round. Top eggplant with a few slices each of mozzarella and tomato. Reduce heat to medium and cover grill or grill pan. (If your grill pan doesn't have a cover, use a baking sheet or frying pan big enough to cover it.) Cook until the cheese begins to melt, 2 to 3 minutes. Check the bottom of the crust periodically during cooking to avoid burning.

4. Once the flatbread pizzas have finished cooking, sprinkle with red chili flakes and chopped mint. Cut into wedges and serve hot or at room temperature.

PREP TIME: 25 minutes
TOTAL TIME: 70 minutes
YIELD: One 14-inch pizza
(serves 2 to 4)

Pizza Provençal

This pie's fresh flavors, creamy Brie, and tangy balsamic reduction make me think of that famous French countryside. Cooking the ingredients separately before adding them to the pizza allows for a unique layering of flavors, a technique made famous by the American queen of French cooking, Julia Child.

Flour for baking sheet and rolling

3 tablespoons olive oil, divided

1 red onion, thinly sliced

6 fingerling potatoes, thinly sliced lengthwise

¼ cup balsamic vinegar

½ recipe pizza dough

3 ounces creamy Brie

6 to 8 fresh sage leaves, torn

Salt and freshly ground black pepper

RECOMMENDED DOUGHS: *Basic, Sourdough, Egg, Gluten-Free*

1. Preheat the oven to 425°F. Lightly flour a baking sheet or pizza pan and set aside.

2. Heat 1 tablespoon of the olive oil in a medium frying pan over medium heat. Add the onion and cook slowly, stirring occasionally, allowing to caramelize, 18 to 20 minutes.

3. Meanwhile, heat another tablespoon of olive oil in a medium frying pan over medium-high heat. Add the potato slices and cook for 3 to 4 minutes on each side, or until golden brown. Remove from heat and set aside.

4. Pour the balsamic vinegar into a small pot and cook over medium heat for 12 to 15 minutes, stirring frequently, allowing to reduce into a thick syrup. Remove from heat.

5. To assemble the pizza, roll the dough out onto another floured surface, making a 14-inch round. Transfer to the prepared baking sheet. Brush dough with the remaining tablespoon olive oil. Arrange onions, Brie, potatoes, and sage evenly over dough and season with salt and pepper. Bake until the cheese melts and the crust is golden brown, 15 to 18 minutes.

6. Before serving, dip a spoon in the balsamic reduction and carefully drizzle reduction over the pizza. Cut into wedges and serve.

Fig and Caramelized Onion Pizza

Here, the heat of the oven gently draws out the figs' sugars, yielding an experience reminiscent of eating pizza with perfect little bites of fig jam. This pizza is intentionally light on cheese so as to accentuate the other delicious toppings.

Flour for baking sheet and rolling

1 tablespoon extra-virgin olive oil

1 small white onion, sliced

1 medium tomato, diced

3 cloves garlic, minced

1 small bunch basil leaves, chopped

Salt and freshly ground black pepper

½ recipe pizza dough

½ cup fontina cheese, shredded

6 fresh Black Mission figs, sliced

RECOMMENDED DOUGHS: *Basic, Honey Whole-Wheat, Sourdough, Gluten-Free*

1. Preheat the oven to 475°F. Lightly flour a baking sheet or pizza pan and set aside.

2. Heat the olive oil in a medium frying pan over medium-low heat. Add the onion slices and allow to cook slowly, stirring infrequently, until they caramelize, 18 to 20 minutes.

3. In a small bowl, combine the tomato, garlic, and basil. Season with salt and pepper. Set aside.

4. On another lightly floured surface, roll the dough out into a 10-inch round. Transfer to the prepared baking sheet. Spread the tomato mixture over the dough, leaving a 1-inch border for the crust. Follow with the cheese. Top with fig slices and caramelized onions.

5. Bake until the crust is crisp and the cheese is melted and brown, 12 to 15 minutes. Cut into wedges and serve.

Green Pizza

I live in the land of upscale pizzerias. Beautiful artisan crusts are topped with organic, local ingredients, baked to perfection and delivered to your table by sexy, tattooed staff. But one of these amazing pies can set you back a cool $20. So stay in with your sexy (tattooed or otherwise) dining companion and whip up an upscale pizza of your own for half the price.

Flour for baking sheet and rolling

½ recipe pizza dough

1 small bunch (handful) flat-leaf parsley leaves

3 scallions, chopped

5 sun-dried tomatoes (see Note)

2 cloves garlic

2 tablespoons extra-virgin olive oil

2 tablespoons grated Parmesan, plus more for sprinkling

Salt and freshly ground black pepper

2 ounces fresh mozzarella (mozzarella di bufala), sliced into medallion-size pieces

1 cup fresh spinach leaves, rinsed and dried

1 small bunch (about 5 stalks) broccolini or baby broccoli

RECOMMENDED DOUGHS: *Basic, Pumpkin, Honey Whole-Wheat, Sourdough, Gluten-Free*

1. Preheat the oven to 475°F. Lightly flour a baking sheet or pizza pan and set aside.

2. On another lightly floured surface, roll the dough into a 12-inch round (or another shape). Transfer to the prepared baking sheet. Set aside.

3. In a food processor or blender, combine parsley, scallions, sun-dried tomatoes, garlic, olive oil, and Parmesan. Season with salt and pepper. Pulse until a chunky pesto forms and then spread over the prepared dough. Top with mozzarella slices and scatter the spinach and broccolini evenly over all. Top with a light sprinkle of Parmesan and a few grinds of pepper.

4. Bake until the crust is golden brown and the cheese starts to bubble, 8 to 10 minutes. Slice into wedges and serve.

Note: *Look for dry, rather than soaked in oil, sun-dried tomatoes, available in the bulk section of most grocers.*

Coppa-Spinach Piadinas

Honestly, this recipe came about one night because I had some beautiful coppa in my fridge, but I couldn't decide between having it on a salad or in a sandwich for dinner. I wanted both. Then I remembered a dish I had several years ago at Cafe Reverie in San Francisco. It was basically a very thin pizza crust topped with a pile of perfectly dressed greens and a light sprinkle of salty cheese—both a sandwich and salad—a compromise in the most delicious sense.

Flour for baking sheet and rolling

½ recipe pizza dough

1 tablespoon extra-virgin olive oil, plus more for brushing

Salt

4 cups fresh spinach, washed and dried

1 tablespoon balsamic vinegar

4 ounces coppa, thinly sliced (prosciutto or salami also work)

1 Roma tomato, sliced

¼ red onion, thinly sliced

2 tablespoons Parmesan, shaved

RECOMMENDED DOUGHS: *Basic, Sourdough, Gluten-Free*

1. Preheat the oven to 475°F. Lightly flour two baking sheets or pizza pans and set aside.

2. Divide the dough into 2 equal balls. Roll out each ball into an 8-inch round.

3. Transfer the rounds to the prepared pans. Brush lightly with olive oil and sprinkle with salt. Bake until the dough looks like a pizza crust, with light brown spots, 8 to 10 minutes.

4. Toss the spinach with the balsamic vinegar and 1 tablespoon of the olive oil.

5. To assemble the piadinas, arrange half of the flatbread with layers of meat, tomato, and onion. Top with half of the dressed spinach and half of the Parmesan. Gently fold over. Repeat with remaining ingredients. Slice each piadina in half to serve.

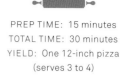

PREP TIME: 15 minutes
TOTAL TIME: 30 minutes
YIELD: One 12-inch pizza
(serves 3 to 4)

Curried Pumpkin Pizza

This unique vegetarian pizza uses curried pumpkin in place of traditional tomato sauce, making for a light-yet-hearty meal. Serve as an appetizer with an earthy ale or lambic beer or with a bowl of soup for lunch or dinner.

Flour for baking sheet and rolling

1 tablespoon extra-virgin olive oil

½ red onion, sliced

1½ cups (12 ounces) canned pumpkin

¾ teaspoon curry powder

1 tablespoon brown sugar

Salt and freshly ground black pepper

½ recipe pizza dough

2 ounces white cheddar or aged Jack cheese

2 cups washed and dried baby spinach leaves

1 jalapeño, sliced into rounds

1 handful fresh cilantro leaves, chopped

RECOMMENDED DOUGHS: *Basic, Pumpkin, Honey Whole-Wheat, Gluten-Free*

1. Preheat the oven to 475°F. Lightly flour a baking sheet or pizza pan and set aside.

2. Heat the olive oil in a medium frying pan over medium heat. Add the onion and cook slowly, stirring occasionally, allowing to caramelize, 18 to 20 minutes. Remove from heat.

3. In a mixing bowl, combine the pumpkin, curry powder, and brown sugar. Season with salt and pepper. Mix well.

4. On another lightly floured surface, roll the pizza dough out into a 12-inch round. Transfer to the prepared baking sheet and spread with the pumpkin mixture, leaving a 1-inch border for the crust. Use a sharp knife or cheese slicer to slice the cheese into about 8 very thin pieces. Scatter over the pumpkin mixture. Top the cheese with the spinach, jalapeño, caramelized onions, and more black pepper.

5. Bake until the crust is golden brown and the cheese begins to bubble, 10 to 12 minutes. Sprinkle with chopped cilantro, cut into wedges, and serve.

PREP TIME: 20 minutes
TOTAL TIME: 50 minutes
YIELD: One 12-inch deep dish pizza
(serves 3 to 4)

Basic Deep-Dish Pizza I discovered deep-dish pizza later in life.

Until a couple of years ago, I believed that the only kind of pizza worth eating was the crisp, lightly topped thin-crust variety, of which I am so fond. Boy, was I wrong.

Deep-dish pizza is a totally different animal. With a thick-yet-crisp cornmeal-coated crust and an almost lasagna-like center, it must be eaten with a knife and fork. Also, the oil called for to grease the pan is imperative—the bottom of the crust essentially fries in the hot oven, yielding a sturdy base for the cheesy, juicy toppings.

Please note that it is nearly impossible to look pretty while eating deep-dish pizza. Eat this with someone who already likes you.

2 tablespoons extra-virgin olive oil

Flour for rolling

1 recipe pizza dough

3 tablespoons cornmeal

1½ cups marinara sauce, divided

1 cup shredded mozzarella cheese

Salt and freshly ground black pepper

RECOMMENDED DOUGHS: *Basic, Honey Whole-Wheat, Gluten-Free*

1. Preheat the oven to 450°F. Pour the oil into an 8-inch cast-iron or oven-proof heavy-bottomed pan. Swirl the oil around to ensure the entire bottom and edges of the pan are coated.

2. On a lightly floured surface, use your hands to pat the dough into a 10-inch round. Sprinkle the cornmeal over the top of the dough and gently press down to adhere the cornmeal to the dough. Carefully transfer the pizza dough, cornmeal-side-down, to the prepared pan. Press the dough into the contours of the pan.

3. Spoon 1 cup of the sauce over the dough. Top with the cheese, season with salt and pepper, and add the remainder of the sauce.

4. Bake until the crust is very crisp and begins to come away from the edges, 26 to 28 minutes. The cheese should be melted and bubbly. Let cool for 5 minutes, cut into wedges, and serve.

Deep-Dish Pizza with Spinach and Prosciutto

This sophisticated, flavorful version of deep-dish pizza was inspired by one I had at San Francisco's Little Star Pizza. Salty prosciutto is nicely balanced by fresh spinach and a generous, but not overwhelming, sprinkle of cheese.

Extra virgin olive oil

Flour for rolling

1 recipe pizza dough

3 tablespoons cornmeal

⅔ cup tomato sauce (Roasted Tomato Sauce, page 12, is great in this recipe)

1 cup shredded mozzarella cheese

3 slices prosciutto, chopped

¼ red onion, chopped

2 cups fresh spinach leaves

Salt and freshly ground black pepper

RECOMMENDED DOUGHS: *Basic, Honey Whole-Wheat, Gluten-Free*

1. Heat the oven to 450°F. Pour 2 tablespoons oil into an 8-inch cast-iron or oven-proof heavy-bottomed pan. Swirl the oil around to ensure the entire bottom and edges of the pan are coated.

2. On a lightly floured surface, use your hands to pat the dough into a 10-inch round. Sprinkle the cornmeal over the top of the dough and gently press down to adhere the cornmeal to the dough. Carefully transfer the pizza dough, cornmeal-side-down, to the prepared pan. Press the dough into the contours of the pan.

3. Spoon the sauce over the dough. Top with the cheese, prosciutto, and onion. Coat the spinach with oil and put on top of the rest of the ingredients. Season with salt and pepper. (Go easy on the salt; the prosciutto is very salty.)

4. Bake until the crust is very crisp and begins to come away from the edges, 26 to 28 minutes. The cheese should be melted and bubbly. Let cool for 5 minutes, cut into wedges, and serve.

South of the Border Deep-Dish Pizza

Prepare 1 recipe pizza dough. Pour prepared salsa or enchilada sauce over the dough and top with shredded Jack cheese and sliced black olives. Bake, according to the Basic Deep-Dish Pizza recipe directions on page 109, and top with guacamole, sour cream, and chopped fresh cilantro, if desired.

RECOMMENDED DOUGHS: *Basic, Honey Whole-Wheat, Sourdough, Gluten-Free*

Spinach-Ricotta Deep-Dish Pizza with Mushrooms

Prepare 1 recipe pizza dough. In a large bowl, stir together 1½ cups ricotta, 10 ounces thawed frozen spinach, 2 cloves minced garlic, ½ finely chopped onion, salt and frehsly ground black pepper to taste. Spoon 1 cup Roasted Tomato Sauce (page 12) onto the prepared deep-dish pizza dough. Top with the ricotta mixture, then add another ½ cup sauce on top. Sprinkle ½ cup thinly sliced mushrooms over the top. Bake according to the Basic Deep-Dish Pizza recipe directions on page 109.

RECOMMENDED DOUGHS: *Basic, Honey Whole-Wheat, Sourdough, Gluten-Free*

Deep-Dish Pesto Pizza with Fresh Arugula

Spread Basil Pesto (page 11) liberally over prepared deep dish pizza dough, leaving a 1-inch border for the crust. Top pesto with sliced buffalo mozzarella medallions, evenly spaced apart. Bake according to the Basic Deep-Dish Pizza recipe directions on page 109. While pizza bakes, dress 2 cups fresh arugula with 1½ table-spoons each extra-virgin olive oil and balsamic vinegar. Season with salt and freshly ground black pepper to taste. Once cooked, cut the pizza into wedges, but leave in the shape of a pizza. Top with the dressed arugula. Serve immediately.

RECOMMENDED DOUGHS:: *Basic, Honey Whole-Wheat, Sourdough, Gluten-Free*

PREP TIME: 20 minutes
TOTAL TIME: 50 minutes
YIELD: Two 8-inch calzones
(serves 3 to 4)

Basic Ricotta Calzones

Calzones are essentially pizzas folded in half, with the internal ingredients getting a lovely steam cooking. Meats stay plump and juicy, vegetables cook just enough to still retain their bold flavors, and cheeses bubble out gorgeously. Make your calzones big and serve one per person, or make them two-bite sized and serve them as an appetizer.

Flour for baking sheet and
   rolling

Extra-virgin olive oil

2 cloves garlic, chopped

2 Roma tomatoes, cored and
   chopped

Salt and freshly ground black
   pepper

1 recipe pizza dough

1 cup fresh ricotta cheese
   (preferable whole cow's
   milk)

RECOMMENDED DOUGHS: *Basic, Herb-Garlic, Honey Whole-Wheat, Sourdough*

1. Preheat the oven to 450°F. Lightly flour a baking sheet and set aside.

2. Heat 2 tablespoons olive oil in a medium frying pan over medium heat. Add the garlic and tomatoes to the pan. Stir to combine and cook for 2 to 3 minutes. Season with salt and pepper. Remove from heat and allow to cool for 5 minutes.

3. On another lightly floured surface, divide the dough into 2 balls. Roll each ball out into an 8-inch round.

4. Spread ¼ cup of the ricotta onto one half of each dough round. Divide the garlic and tomato mixture atop the ricotta and top each with some of the remaining ricotta. Fold the dough over to form half-moons and pinch the edges together to seal.

5. Brush the tops of the calzones with a bit of olive oil and transfer to the prepared baking sheet. Bake until the crust is golden brown, 14 to 16 minutes. Let cool for 5 minutes and then serve.

Pumpkin Carriage

Prepare 1 recipe pizza dough. Simply spread cooked, pureed pumpkin (canned is fine) over the dough and top with white cheddar, caramelized onions, and finely chopped sage. Bake according to the Basic Ricotta Calzone recipe directions on page 113 and top with lots of freshly ground black pepper.

RECOMMENDED DOUGH: *Pumpkin*

Moon over Parma

Prepare 1 recipe pizza dough. Spread tomato sauce over the dough and top with shredded fontina and Asiago cheeses. Top with thin slices of Parma ham and bake according to the Basic Ricotta Calzone recipe directions on page 113. After baking, top with fresh basil or flat-leaf parsley if you want to add a pop of color and bite.

RECOMMENDED DOUGHS: *Basic, Sourdough, Gluten-Free*

From España, with Love

Prepare 1 recipe pizza dough. Simply spread fresh romesco sauce over the dough, top with shredded (or crumbled) Manchego cheese, and then chopped Spanish serrano ham. Bake according to the Basic Ricotta Calzone recipe directions on page 113 and top with chopped, fresh flat-leaf parsley.

RECOMMENDED DOUGHS: *Basic, Sourdough, Gluten-Free*

Meat-Lover's Calzones This calzone is for your inner carnivore.
Don't bother making this one with meat substitutes; it should be assembled as is.

Flour for baking sheet and rolling

Extra-virgin olive oil

¼ onion, chopped

2 cloves garlic, chopped

2 Roma tomatoes, cored and chopped

Salt and freshly ground black pepper

½ pound ground Italian sausage, crumbled, then cooked over medium heat and drained

About 20 slices pepperoni, chopped

½ recipe pizza dough

1 cup fresh ricotta cheese (preferably whole cow's milk)

RECOMMENDED DOUGHS: *Basic, Herb-Garlic, Honey Whole-Wheat, Sourdough*

1. Preheat the oven to 450°F. Lightly flour a baking sheet and set aside.

2. Heat 2 tablespoons olive oil in a medium frying pan over medium heat. Add the onion and cook for 3 to 4 minutes, until it begins to soften. Add the garlic and tomatoes to the pan. Stir to combine. Season with salt and pepper, remove from heat, and allow to cool for 5 minutes.

3. Stir the tomato mixture together with the sausage and pepperoni.

4. On another lightly floured surface, divide the dough into 2 balls. Roll each ball out into a 6-inch round and spread ¼ cup of the ricotta onto half of each dough round. Divide the meat and tomato mixture over the ricotta and top each with some of the remaining ricotta. Fold the dough over to form half-moons and pinch the edges together to seal.

5. Brush the tops of the calzones with a bit of olive oil and transfer them to the prepared baking sheet. Bake until the crust is golden brown, 14 to 16 minutes. Let the calzones cool for 5 minutes and then serve.

PREP TIME: 25 minutes
TOTAL TIME: 50 minutes
YIELD: Four 6-inch calzones
(serves 4)

Pesto-Sausage Calzones

I like to pack these, at room temperature, for a picnic. Enjoyed with a little sangria and a green salad, they are just the thing to munch on al fresco on a warm summer night.

You can also feel free to get creative with the fillings. Swap out the Italian sausage for chorizo and add queso fresco and chopped cilantro for a Mexican twist. Or try cooked, chopped chicken-apple sausage and fresh chopped sage for an autumn treat.

Flour for baking sheet and rolling

2 tablespoons extra-virgin olive oil

1 onion, chopped

3 cloves garlic, chopped

1 cup (packed) fresh spinach

½ cup Fresh Basil Pesto (page 11)

Salt and freshly ground black pepper to taste

½ pound ground Italian sausage, crumbled, then cooked over medium heat and drained

1 recipe pizza dough

1¼ cups fresh ricotta cheese (preferably whole cow's milk)

RECOMMENDED DOUGHS: *Basic, Herb-Garlic, Honey Whole-Wheat, Sourdough*

1. Preheat the oven to 450°F. Lightly flour a baking sheet and set aside.

2. Heat 2 tablespoons olive oil in a medium frying pan over medium heat. Add the onion and cook for 3 to 4 minutes, until it begins to soften. Add the garlic and spinach to the pan. Stir to combine and cook until the spinach completely breaks down, 2 to 3 minutes. Season with salt and pepper. Remove from heat and allow to cool for 5 minutes. Stir together with the cooked sausage.

3. On another lightly floured surface, divide the dough into 4 balls. Roll each ball out into a 6-inch round.

4. Spread ¼ cup of the ricotta onto half of each dough round. Divide the spinach-sausage mixture over the ricotta and top each with some of the remaining ricotta. Fold the dough over to form half-moons and pinch the edges together to seal.

5. Brush the tops of the calzones with a bit of olive oil and transfer them to the prepared baking sheet. Bake until crust is golden brown, 14 to 16 minutes. Let cool for 5 minutes and then serve.

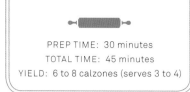

PREP TIME: 30 minutes
TOTAL TIME: 45 minutes
YIELD: 6 to 8 calzones (serves 3 to 4)

Breakfast Calzones

These crisp little pockets of deliciousness are the perfect brunch item, although I like them for lunch and dinner as well. Filled with savory bacon, soft scrambled eggs, and sweet potatoes, they're an easy crowd-pleaser. In a pinch, make them with store-bought pie dough.

2 cups all-purpose flour, plus more for baking sheet and rolling

1 recipe pizza dough

3 slices thick-cut bacon

1 small sweet potato, scrubbed and diced

1 small onion, diced

2 cups spinach leaves

4 eggs, lightly beaten

¼ cup shredded sharp cheddar cheese

1 teaspoon salt

Freshly ground black pepper

RECOMMENDED DOUGHS: *Basic, Honey Whole-Wheat, Rye, Egg*

1. Preheat the oven to 400°F. Lightly flour a baking sheet and set aside.

2. On another lightly floured work surface, use a floured rolling pin to roll dough out into a large round, about ¼ inch thick. Use small bowls or large cups to cut 5- or 6-inch rounds out of the dough. Place on wax or parchment paper until ready to use. You should have 6 to 8 rounds.

3. Heat a large ungreased frying pan over high heat. Cook bacon for 1 to 2 minutes on each side, or until quite crisp. Drain on paper towels. Lower the heat to medium high and cook the sweet potato and onion for 4 to 5 minutes, or until sweet potato begins to soften. Add the spinach and eggs. Cook until eggs are set, stirring frequently. Crumble cooked bacon over mixture and stir in cheddar cheese, salt, and pepper to taste. Scrape mixture into a bowl and allow to cool for 5 minutes.

4. Once mixture has cooled, scoop 3 to 4 tablespoons of the mixture onto each dough round, and fold over, pinching to seal. Transfer calzones to the prepared baking sheet and bake until crusts are golden brown, 12 to 15 minutes. Serve warm.

Note: *This is a great recipe with which to switch up the ingredients. These can easily be made vegetarian. They would also be equally delicious with chorizo and red potatoes in place of the bacon and sweet potatoes.*

Vegetarian Calzone This is a strictly vegetarian variation of the calzone. If you're making this for vegans, add ½ cup of extra sauce and skip the ricotta.

Flour for baking sheet and rolling

Extra-virgin olive oil

¼ onion, chopped

2 cloves garlic, chopped

2 Roma tomatoes, cored and chopped

1 cup (packed) fresh spinach

Salt and freshly ground black pepper

1 recipe pizza dough

½ cup fresh ricotta cheese (preferably whole cow's milk)

RECOMMENDED DOUGHS: *Basic, Herb-Garlic, Pumpkin, Honey Whole-Wheat*

1. Preheat the oven to 450°F. Lightly flour a baking sheet and set aside.

2. Heat 2 tablespoons olive oil in a medium frying pan over medium heat. Add the onion and cook for 3 to 4 minutes, until it begins to soften. Add the garlic, tomatoes, and spinach to the pan. Stir to combine and cook until the spinach completely breaks down, 2 to 3 minutes. Season with salt and pepper. Remove from heat and allow to cool for 5 minutes.

3. On another lightly floured surface, divide the dough into 2 balls. Roll each ball out into an 8-inch round and spread ⅛ cup of the ricotta onto half of each dough round. Spread the tomato-spinach mixture over the ricotta and top each with some of the remaining ricotta. Fold dough over to form half-moons and pinch the edges together to seal.

4. Brush the tops of the calzones with a bit of olive oil and transfer to the prepared baking sheet. Bake until the crust is golden brown, 14 to 16 minutes. Let cool for 5 minutes and then serve.

CHAPTER 5

SWEETS

I've never considered myself much of a baker. There's too much measuring, worrying, and waiting. I'm an instant gratification kind of girl. Fortunately, using pizza dough in desserts is a great way to make impatient cooks like myself feel like successful bakers. It offers a combination of quick assembly, short cooking times, and gorgeous delicious results, from hot, puffy doughnuts to ooey-gooey Glazed Cinnamon Rolls (page 122) to flaky honey-drenched Sopapillas (page 135), and the ultimate comfort dessert, Caramel-Pecan Monkey Bread (page 129). Keep pizza dough in your refrigerator, and you'll never be caught hosting a dinner party—or brunch—without something sweet to include.

Glazed Cinnamon Rolls

If you are hosting a breakfast or brunch, assemble (but don't bake) these cinnamon rolls the night before and then cover the pan with plastic wrap. Then, while you brew coffee in the morning, pop them into the oven to bake for an impressive, hassle-free brunch.

Vegetable oil or cooking spray for greasing baking sheet

2 teaspoons cinnamon

½ cup granulated sugar

Flour for rolling

1 recipe pizza dough

¼ cup (½ stick) unsalted butter, at room temperature, plus 2 tablespoons, melted

½ cup powdered sugar, plus more if desired

1 teaspoon vanilla

2 tablespoons water

RECOMMENDED DOUGH: *Egg*

1. Preheat the oven to 375°F. Lightly grease a baking sheet with vegetable oil or cooking spray and set aside.

2. Mix the cinnamon and granulated sugar in a bowl. Combine well.

3. On a lightly floured surface, roll the pizza dough into a 14-by-10-inch rectangle. Use a spatula to spread 4 tablespoons of the soft butter over the dough, making sure it is entirely covered. Sprinkle the cinnamon-sugar mixture over the butter, again making sure the entire rectangle is covered.

4. Starting at the bottom of the dough, roll the longest way from the bottom to the top until you have a 10-inch cylinder, pinching to seal. Cut the cylinder into ten 1-inch pieces and transfer to the prepared baking sheet.

5. Bake the cinnamon rolls until outsides are golden brown and butter-cinnamon mixture begins to lightly bubble, 12 to 15 minutes. Allow to cool slightly.

6. Whisk together the melted butter, powdered sugar, vanilla, and water until creamy. Add a bit more powdered sugar, if needed, to achieve a smooth glaze. Drizzle the glaze over the warm cinnamon rolls and serve.

Chocolate-Hazelnut Pizza

Surprise your dinner guests by serving pizza at the end of the meal! This beautiful pie features an indulgent combination of Nutella, white, semisweet and milk chocolate, and a pleasant crunch, courtesy of toasted hazelnuts.

To really put this over the top, serve it a la mode.

1 recipe pizza dough

2 teaspoons butter, melted

¼ cup chocolate-hazelnut spread (such as Nutella)

½ cup semisweet chocolate chips

2 tablespoons milk chocolate chips

2 tablespoons white chocolate chips

2 tablespoons chopped hazelnuts, toasted (see Note, page 29)

¼ teaspoon sea salt, or to taste

RECOMMENDED DOUGH: *Chocolate*

1. Position an oven rack on the bottom of the oven and preheat to 450°F. Line a heavy, large baking sheet with parchment paper and set aside.

2. On a lightly floured surface, roll out the dough to a 9-inch round and then transfer the dough to the prepared baking sheet. Using your fingers, make indentations all over the dough and brush with the butter.

3. Bake until the crust is crisp and pale golden brown, about 20 minutes. Immediately layer the chocolate-hazelnut spread over the pizza and sprinkle the chocolate chips over the top. Bake again, just until the chocolate begins to melt, about 1 minute.

4. Sprinkle the hazelnuts and sea salt over the pizza. Cut into wedges and serve.

PREP TIME: 55 minutes
TOTAL TIME: 1 hour, 10 minutes
YIELD: 12 to 14 spirals
(serves 12 to 14)

Pumpkin Pie Spirals

Enjoy these plain or with icing. Personally, I think they're moist enough to go without icing, but if you're an icing person, whisk together 2 tablespoons milk, ½ cup powdered sugar, and a few drops of vanilla and drizzle it over these fall all-stars.

1 recipe pizza dough

¼ cup (½ stick) butter, at room temperature

½ cup (4 ounces) cream cheese, at room temperature

¾ cup brown sugar

1½ teaspoons pumpkin pie spice (see Note)

RECOMMENDED DOUGH: *Pumpkin*

1. Preheat the oven to 375°F. Lightly flour a baking sheet and set aside.

2. On another lightly floured surface, roll the dough out into a large rectangle (about 12-by-16 inches).

3. In a small bowl, combine the butter, cream cheese, and sugar. Stir in the pumpkin pie spice.

4. Use a rubber spatula or butter knife to spread the butter-sugar mixture all over the expanse of the dough. Roll up tightly, pinching to seal, so you have a 10-inch-long cylinder.

5. Use a sharp knife to carefully cut the cylinder into 12 to 14 half-inch disks. Arrange the disks on the prepared baking sheet.

6. Bake until the edges have turned golden brown, 13 to 16 minutes. Let cool slightly and serve warm.

Note: *If you don't have pumpkin pie spice, but you do have cinnamon, nutmeg, and ginger, use a mixture of those instead.*

PREP TIME: 20 minutes
TOTAL TIME: 40 minutes
YIELD: One 12-inch pizza
(serves 6 to 8)

Oreo Cookie Pizza

Want to be the favorite mom/dad/aunt/babysitter of all the kids you know? Make this pizza for them. It's a sugar fest, packaged in a fun-to-eat pizza pie. For even more fun, put out the dough, toppings, and a baking sheet and let the kids build it themselves.

1 recipe pizza dough

1 cup miniature marshmallows

6 Oreos (or other chocolate sandwich cookies), roughly chopped

⅓ cup chopped walnuts or pecans

⅓ cup candy-coated chocolate pieces or peanut butter candies

RECOMMENDED DOUGHS: *Chocolate, Egg*

1. Preheat the oven to 350°F. On a lightly floured surface, roll the dough out into a 12-inch round.

2. Press the pizza dough into a greased 12-inch pizza pan. Bake until firm, 10 to 12 minutes.

3. Sprinkle the marshmallows over the crust and return to oven. Bake 3 to 5 minutes more, until the marshmallows are lightly browned.

4. Top with the chopped Oreos, nuts, and candies, pressing them lightly into the softened marshmallow. Cool slightly before slicing and serving.

PREP TIME: 1 hour
TOTAL TIME: 1 hour, 30 minutes
YIELD: 1 loaf wreath (serves 6 to 8).

Caramel-Pecan Monkey Bread

Will I be stripped of my "Nice Jewish Girl" status if I tell you that the Moskowitz family actually has some pretty sweet Christmas traditions? We are spiritually, religiously, and culturally Jewish, and so we do the usual Chinese-food-and-a-movie thing on Christmas Eve along with all the other Israelites in my hometown of Santa Rosa, California. But after that, it's Moskowitz Secular Christmastime!

After our chop suey and egg rolls, we head back to my parents' house, where my mom gives all of us a special Christmas Eve. We put on our new pajamas, sip spiked eggnog, and listen to my father play the piano. In the morning, we exchange presents and eat an extravagant breakfast courtesy of my mom, that consists of mimosas, coffee, eggs, and monkey bread—a lovely, sticky, caramel-y combination of fluffy biscuits, cinnamon, melted brown sugar, and butter. Lots of butter.

1 cup pecan halves

1 cup (packed) dark brown sugar

3 teaspoons ground cinnamon

1 teaspoon salt

1 cup (2 sticks) melted butter

1 recipe pizza dough

Flour for rolling

RECOMMENDED DOUGH: *Egg*

1. Preheat the oven to 350°F. Grease a 6-cup Bundt pan liberally and set aside.

2. Sprinkle 1/3 of the pecan halves directly into the greased pan.

3. Meanwhile, combine the brown sugar, cinnamon, and salt in a bowl. Stir well and set aside. Set the melted butter in a bowl next to the brown sugar–cinnamon mixture.

4. Turn the dough out onto a lightly floured surface and use your hands to pat it into a 6-by-8-inch rectangle. Use a sharp knife to cut the dough into about 48 one-inch squares.

continued

5. To form the bread, lightly flour your hands. Pick up a square and roll it gently between your hands until you have a round ball. Dip each ball in the butter and then immediately into the brown sugar–cinnamon mixture and place it in the prepared pan. Sprinkle another $1/3$ of the pecan halves over the top. Continue with the remaining dough, butter, and brown sugar–cinnamon mixture, piling the balls on top of each other in sort of a stacked wreath. Top with the remaining $1/3$ of the pecan halves. Cover loosely with plastic wrap and let rise in a warm spot for 15 minutes.

6. Remove plastic wrap and bake until brown and sticky, 25 to 30 minutes.

7. To serve, flip the Bundt pan over and transfer to a serving plate or platter. Serve immediately.

Fried Apple Pies

A tradition in the south, fried apple pies are an indulgent but worthwhile occasional treat! When made with pizza dough, they yield a doughnut-pie hybrid, impossible to turn down. These make a great finish to a backyard barbecue.

2 pounds Granny Smith apples, peeled, cored, and thinly sliced

2 cups sugar

2 tablespoons cinnamon

1 recipe pizza dough

Vegetable oil for frying

1 to 1½ cups powdered sugar

RECOMMENDED DOUGHS: *Basic, Egg*

1. Place the apples in a large pot and add enough water to barely cover them. Add the sugar and cinnamon. Bring the mixture to a boil over medium heat. Cook until tender, stirring occasionally, about 15 minutes. The apples should be soft and the syrup around them thick.

2. On a floured surface, divide the pizza dough into 15 pieces. Roll each piece into a very thin round—very thin. (It is best to do no more than six at a time). Place approximately 2 tablespoons of the apple mixture in the center of each biscuit. Fold over into a half-moon shape and press edges together firmly.

3. Pour about 3 inches of vegetable oil into a large heavy-bottomed pot. If necessary, add more oil during frying. Heat over medium-high heat to about 300°F. Working in batches, fry the pies until golden brown on both sides. Remove the pies from the pot and place on paper towels to drain. Let cool.

4. As pies cool, make the glaze, taking 1 to 1½ cups powdered, sugar and adding enough water to make the mixture thin enough to drizzle on the pies. Drizzle glaze on the pies and serve.

PREP TIME: 30 minutes
TOTAL TIME: 55 minutes
YIELD: 10 to 12 turnovers
(serves 10 to 12)

Raspberry Pastry Turnovers

These sweet, raspberry-filled squares straddle the line of breakfast and dessert. They could easily be served with coffee, fruit, and scrambled eggs as part of a fancy brunch, or with a scoop of sorbet or gelato at the end of a meal.

1 recipe pizza dough

½ cup (4 ounces) cream cheese, room temperature

1 egg yolk

½ cup powdered sugar

½ teaspoon vanilla extract

½ teaspoon grated lemon zest

1 egg

1 tablespoon water

½ pint raspberries

2 teaspoons granulated sugar

RECOMMENDED DOUGHS: *Basic, Egg*

1. Preheat the oven to 375°F. On a lightly floured surface, roll the dough out into an 11-by-14-inch rectangle.

2. Using a mixer with a paddle attachment, an electric beater, or a whisk, mix the cream cheese, egg yolk, powdered sugar, vanilla extract, and lemon zest until creamy and combined.

3. Make an egg wash by whisking together the egg and the water in a small bowl. Cut the dough into 3-inch squares (you should have 20 to 24 squares). Lay a square of dough on a lightly floured work surface and paint the edge with egg wash. In the center of the pastry, place 1 tablespoon of the cheese filling and 3 raspberries. Paint the edge of a second square of pastry with egg wash, place it on top of the filling, and carefully press the edges together to seal them well. Place the turnovers 1 inch apart on a parchment paper–lined baking sheet. Repeat with the remaining dough.

4. When all of the turnovers have been formed, brush their top surfaces with the remaining egg wash and sprinkle with sugar. Bake until golden brown, 20 to 25 minutes. Serve warm.

Sopapillas

The sopapilla is a delicious, easy dessert that goes nicely with Latin American fare. If you have a deep fryer, use it to make these. If not, shallow-frying them in a heavy pot or frying pan will do just fine. I like to serve these hot with cinnamon coffee.

Flour for rolling

1 recipe pizza dough

Vegetable oil for frying

Powdered sugar for dusting

Honey for serving

RECOMMENDED DOUGH: *Egg*

1. On a lightly floured surface, roll the pizza dough out to about ¼ inch thick. Use a knife to cut the dough into about 20 three-inch squares.

2. Heat about 1 inch of vegetable oil in a deep pot or frying pan. Fry dough a few pieces at a time, turning them over as needed to allow the sopapillas to cook evenly. Fry until golden brown on both sides. Drain on paper towels.

3. Dust with powdered sugar and serve hot with honey drizzled over or alongside.

PREP TIME: 25 minutes
TOTAL TIME: 1 hour
YIELD: 10 to 12 doughnuts
(serves 10 to 12)

Glazed Lemon Curd Doughnuts

Store-bought lemon curd works overtime to make these pretty little doughnuts look a whole lot more complicated than they actually are. I like to serve them with mint tea or afternoon coffee.

Flour for rolling

1 recipe pizza dough

⅔ cup lemon curd, divided

Vegetable oil for frying

½ cup powdered sugar, plus more for dusting

¼ cup cream cheese, room temperature

Zest and juice of 1 lemon

RECOMMENDED DOUGH: *Egg*

1. On a lightly floured surface, roll the dough out to about ½ inch thick. Use a small juice glass, wineglass, or small biscuit cutter to cut the dough into 2-inch rounds. Gather scraps and re-roll until all the dough has been cut into rounds (you should have 20 to 24 rounds).

2. Place 2 to 3 teaspoons lemon curd in the center of a round of dough. Dip your finger in water and lightly run it around the edge of the circle. Cover with a second round of dough and gently fold the edge of the lower circle of dough over the upper circle to seal tightly. Repeat with remaining dough rounds.

3. Pour about 2 inches of vegetable oil into a large pot. Heat over medium-high heat to about 375°F. (If you don't have a thermometer, check readiness by dropping a small piece of dough into the bubbling oil; the oil is ready when the dough quickly puffs and browns.) Working in batches, fry the doughnuts until brown and puffy. (Watch them the whole time that they cook.) Use tongs to carefully flip them as necessary. Remove cooked doughnuts from the hot oil using tongs and drain on paper towels. Let cool.

4. Whisk together ½ cup powdered sugar, ¼ cup lemon curd, the softened cream cheese, and the lemon juice. Add a couple teaspoons of water if necessary to create a thick glaze and continue whisking until all the lumps have dissolved.

5. Dip each doughnut in the glaze (or use a butter knife to spread it over the top) and sprinkle a tiny pinch of zest across the top and serve.

PREP TIME: 30 minutes
TOTAL TIME: 50 minutes
YIELD: 10 to 12 doughnuts
(serves 10 to 12)

Jelly Doughnuts

Usually, when I bite into a doughnut and find that it contains jelly on the inside, I am annoyed by the gelatinous goo getting in the way of my light and fluffy doughnut. Sufganiyot, however, are a different story.

These special Hanukkah doughnuts are best served warm, with a lightly crisp exterior and plenty of powdered sugar. I like to place a dot of jelly or jam atop the sugary confection to prepare guests for its fruity interior.

Flour for rolling

1 recipe pizza dough

1 cup jelly or jam of your choice

Vegetable or canola oil for frying

Powdered sugar for dusting

RECOMMENDED DOUGHS: *Basic, Egg*

1. On a lightly floured surface, roll the dough out to about ½ inch thick. Use a small juice glass, wineglass, or small biscuit cutter to cut the dough into 2-inch rounds. Gather scraps and re-roll until all the dough has been cut into rounds (you should have 20 to 24 rounds).

2. Place 2 to 3 teaspoons jelly in the center of a round of dough. Dip your finger in water and lightly run it around the edge of the circle. Cover with a second round of dough and gently fold the edge of the lower circle of dough over the upper circle to seal tightly. Repeat with remaining dough rounds.

3. Pour about 2 inches of vegetable oil into a large pot. Heat over medium-high heat to about 375°F. (If you don't have a thermometer, check readiness by dropping a small piece of dough into the bubbling oil; the oil is ready when the dough quickly puffs and browns.) Working in batches, fry the doughnuts until brown and puffy. (Watch them the whole time that they cook.) Use tongs to carefully flip them as necessary.

4. Remove the cooked doughnuts from the hot oil using tongs and drain on paper towels. Let the doughnuts cool until warm (not hot) to the touch. Dust with powdered sugar and top each doughnut with a dot of jelly. Serve warm.

PREP TIME: 25 minutes
TOTAL TIME: 40 minutes
YIELD: 8 large pretzels (serves 8)

Dessert Pretzels

Looking for some delicious, indoor fun? Try your hand at making sweet, soft pretzels. They are super easy to make with store-bought pizza dough, and it's a great activity for the kids—forming the twisty shape is a fun activity for little helpers.

Oil or cooking spray for greasing the pan

1 recipe pizza dough

Flour for dusting

⅔ cup semisweet mini chocolate chips (or use the equivalent finely chopped semisweet chocolate)

3 tablespoons baking soda

2 tablespoons coarse sugar

RECOMMENDED DOUGHS: *Basic, Honey Whole-Wheat, Chocolate*

1. Preheat the oven to 475°F. Lightly grease a baking sheet and set aside.

2. Place the dough on a lightly floured work surface. Sprinkle with chocolate chips and gently knead to incorporate.

3. Divide the dough into 8 equal pieces and roll each piece into a 12-inch-long rope. To shape the dough into pretzels, form each dough rope into a "U" shape and twist ends twice. Fold the twisted ends down and pinch to seal. Transfer pretzels to the prepared baking sheet and let rest for 20 minutes.

4. Bring a large pot of water to a boil and add the baking soda. In batches, boil pretzels until puffed and slightly shiny, about 1 minute. With a slotted spoon, transfer them to a wire rack to drain.

5. Return the pretzels to the baking sheet and sprinkle with the sugar. Bake until golden brown and cooked through, 10 to 15 minutes, rotating the sheet halfway through. Serve warm or at room temperature.

Index

⊠ EGG&DART.PRESS